THE K

HAN

WILDLIFE

OF BRITAIN & EUROPE

JEANNETTE HARRIS

KINGfISHER

ADVISERS:
Michael Chinery
Naturalist, writer and broadcaster

Esmond Harris
*Director of the Royal Forestry
Society*

Richard Mabey
Writer, botanist and broadcaster

Peter Olney
*Curator of Birds, Zoological
Society, London*

Derek Reid
*Head of Mycology Department,
Royal Botanic Gardens, Kew*

KINGFISHER
An imprint of Larousse plc
New Penderel House
283-288 High Holborn
London WC1V 7HZ

First published as *Nature Handbook*
in 1981
This edition published in 1998

10 9 8 7 6 5 4 3 2 1

Copyright © Larousse plc 1998

ISBN 0 7534 0245 9

Printed in Spain

Contents

Introduction

Learning about nature begins with looking – with noticing the differences between one tree, bird, flower, insect or fish and another. The *Pocket Guide* will help you to do this, and to identify those plants or animals you are most likely to see in Britain and northern Europe. In the book, which includes over 700 species, a wide variety of plants – trees, flowers and non-green plants or fungi – are illustrated and described, as well as many animals, including mammals, birds, fishes, seashore creatures, insects, amphibians and reptiles.

Each species is identified by its common as well as its scientific name. The common names can be confusing as there are often several for one plant or animal, and sometimes one name can apply to several different species. To avoid confusion, scientists have developed rules governing the use of scientific names. These are often called Latin names, but this is inaccurate, as some of the words are Greek. In scientific language, every species has a name made up of two parts. The first part is the 'generic' name e.g., *Pinus* (a pine

◀ The bumblebee is one of the many insects which pollinate flowering plants. The pollen sticks to the bee's fur and is later gathered by the bee into 'pollen baskets' on the hind legs.

▶ All plants and animals have adapted to make use of a particular habitat. Here alder thrives in wet conditions because it has special bacteria growing in root nodules which help it to live in waterlogged conditions.

tree) and is common to all pines. The second is the 'specific' name which refers to one species only e.g., *P. sylvestris*, Scots pine (which, despite its common name in English, is abundant throughout northern Europe and Scandinavia). The index includes both common and scientific names.

Unless otherwise stated, the measurements given are the total length of the animal or the height of the plant. All measurements are the normal average of a mature plant or animal and are only a guide, as individuals can vary greatly. Colour and markings also vary. There are often colour differences between young and mature and, more often, between male and female of the same species. The symbols ♂ denoting male and ♀ denoting female are used throughout the book where there is a significant difference between the two.

Each area supports a particular network of wildlife, depending on its climate and geography. Different types of soil produce different plants, these plants are eaten by certain animals and these animals will be the food of other animals. In this way, a whole chain of life is set up, adapted to the environment or habitat – be it field, wood, marsh, river, mountain or coastline. Whichever part of the country you live in, you will gradually learn to know which plants and animals to expect there, and to trace the relationship between them.

Mammals

Mammals are a distinct group of animals that feed their young on milk secreted by special glands. The young are cared for by their mothers until they are old enough to look after themselves. Most mammals have hair, both soft under-fur to keep them warm and coarse outer hair, which helps to repel rain and keep the animal dry.

Mammals are divided into groups or orders according to their body structure and the way they live. The mammals in this book belong to the following orders:

The rodents (vole, mouse, rat, squirrel, coypu). These mammals have large incisor (front) teeth, specially adapted for gnawing, which grow throughout their life. Most of these mammals are small and breed quickly, producing large numbers of young.

The insect-eaters (mole, hedgehog, shrew) have lots of small, pointed teeth for eating and crushing the insects and other small creatures on which they feed.

▼ **Badger** *Meles meles* 75–93cm. Immensely strong for its size, with a tenacious grip. Found nearly all over Europe.

The meat-eaters (fox, badger, otter, mink, stoat, weasel, polecat, marten, wild cat) have large, pointed 'eye' teeth or canines, used for stabbing and tearing up meat or fish, and powerful jaws.

The hooved mammals (deer, goat, sheep) have divided hooves and are animals which eat grass and other plants. They lack teeth at the front of the upper jaw, where there is a hard pad for the lower teeth to bite on when tearing up grass. The grass is swallowed, then later regurgitated for chewing into smaller fragments. Animals that eat in this way are called ruminants. Goats and sheep of both sexes have horns, but only male deer have antlers, which they shed once a year and regrow. Pigs have hooves but they are not ruminants.

The flying mammals (bats) have wings supported by their limbs. They catch insects in flight by echo-location. They send out high-pitched squeaks and listen for echoes bouncing back from insects.

The seals have teeth like carnivores (meat-eaters), but their limbs have developed as flippers with which to swim. They can stay under water for long periods, rising regularly to the surface to breathe.

The dolphins and porpoises are adapted to living completely in water. Their bodies are streamlined for fast swimming.

▼ **Chamois** *Rupicapra rupicapra* 110–130cm. Goat-like, with small, slender horns curved at the tips, and white markings. Lives in mountains in Europe.

CLUES AND HINTS

Food remains and droppings: Look out for cones attacked by squirrels, nuts gnawed by mice, fish bitten by otters. Deer and rabbit droppings are easily identified.
Animal homes: Look out for squirrel dreys in the forks of trees, rabbit holes and badger sets.
Sounds: Listen for the bark of a roe-deer, the high-pitched squeak of a shrew or bat.
Tracks: Look out for broad pads (badger) and oval ones (fox). Position varies if walking or running. (See page 8.)
Other signs: Shed antlers or frayed trees show that deer are about. Hairs caught in a fence can be identified with practice.

Measurements given are the total length of head, body and tail, though the length of tail is given separately where it is significant. Where appropriate the height to the shoulder is given. All measurements are averages and only a guide, as individuals vary greatly in size. Colour and markings also vary, and young animals are often very different from adults and are, of course, smaller.

Mammals are more difficult to observe than other animals as many are shy, small and only active at night or in the early morning. There is still a great deal to be found out about their habits and behaviour by the careful and patient amateur observer.

TRACKS

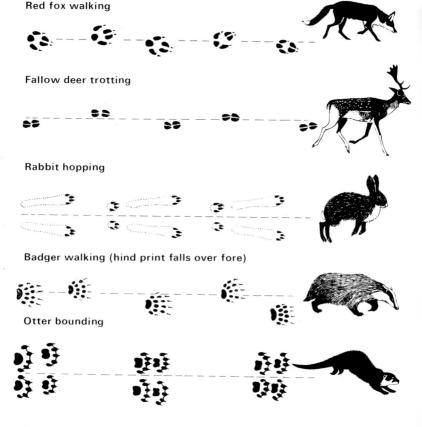

Red fox walking

Fallow deer trotting

Rabbit hopping

Badger walking (hind print falls over fore)

Otter bounding

Rabbit, Hares and Rodents

▶ **Rabbit** *Oryctolagus cuniculus*
35–45cm. Long ears, no black tips
like hares. Long hind legs. White tail,
easily seen when rabbit moves. Colour
greyish-brown, white below,
sometimes black. Hops, thumps back
legs when alarmed. Lives in groups
in burrows.

◀ **Brown Hare** *Lepus capensis*
48–67cm. Long ears with black
tips. Light sandy-brown in colour,
white underparts. Larger than
rabbit with longer legs, so lopes
rather than hops. When disturbed,
runs very quickly, twisting and
turning. Fields and open country.

▶ **Mountain Hare** *Lepus timidus*
45–50cm. Black-tipped ears are
shorter than brown hare, smaller
and more rabbit-like. Grey in summer,
turns white in winter except for ear
tips. Mainly in upland areas.

▲ **Coypu** *Myocastor coypus* 42–
60cm. Like large guinea pig with long
thick tail. Often seen swimming when
blunt nose, broad head and back show
above the water. Webbed hind feet.
Active dawn and dusk. Burrows in
river banks.

▶ **Muskrat** *Ondatra zibethicus* 26–
35cm. Tail flattened from side to side
for swimming. Active night and early
morning in still and slow-moving
water with lots of weeds. Not in
Britain.

Rodents

◄ **Grey Squirrel** *Sciurus carolinensis*
Body 25—30cm, tail 20cm. Head
broader and more rat-like than red
squirrel. Summer coat is grey, with
red-brown on the flanks and white
underparts, winter coat grey, tail dark
grey. Some animals have more red-
brown in the coat than others. Ear tufts
not noticeable. Builds dreys in trees.
Mainly deciduous woods and
parklands.

▶ **Red Squirrel** *Sciurus vulgaris*
Body 20—22cm, tail 20cm. Smaller,
with narrower head than grey squirrel.
Tail bushier, becoming very light in
summer. Coat becomes greyer and ear
tufts longer during the winter. Darker
specimens in southern Europe. Prefers
woods with conifers, feeding on
shoots and cones.

◄ **Short-tailed Vole** *Microtus
agrestis* Body 9—12cm, tail 3—4cm.
Coat brown above, grey below. Rough
grassland, including moors and
marshes, and light woodland.
Sometimes in large numbers. Common.

◄ **Water Vole** *Arvicola terrestris*
Body 17—20cm, tail 9—12cm. Swims
with broad flat head and blunt nose
just above the water. Lives by and in
water.

▶ **Bank Vole** *Clethrionomys
glareolus* Body 9—12cm, tail 4—7cm.
Rich red-brown upper parts, creamy-
white underparts. Deciduous
woodland, hedgerows and gardens.

◀ **Wood Mouse** *Apodemus sylvaticus* Body 9cm, tail 8cm. Pointed muzzle, large eyes, ears and hind feet. Underparts grey or white, often with yellowish spot on chest. Nocturnal. Common.

◀ **Harvest Mouse** *Micromys minutus* Body 5–7cm, tail 6–7cm. Muzzle not pointed like other mice, head broader. Tail used for holding on to vegetation. Active mainly by day in tall, rough grassland and in cornfields.

◀ **House Mouse** *Mus musculus* Body 7–8cm, tail 7–8cm. Long pointed nose. Fur grey. Leaves a characteristic 'mousey' smell where present. Mainly nocturnal. Rarely far from man.

▶ **Dormouse** *Muscardinus avellanarius* Body 7cm, tail 6cm. Tail hairy unlike those of voles and mice. Hibernates October to April. Deciduous woodland, hedges.

▶ **Edible Dormouse** *Glis glis* Body 17cm, tail 15cm. Like young grey squirrel, but head mouse-like with bulging eyes. Nocturnal, lives in trees.

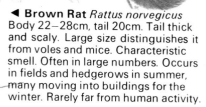

◀ **Brown Rat** *Rattus norvegicus* Body 22–28cm, tail 20cm. Tail thick and scaly. Large size distinguishes it from voles and mice. Characteristic smell. Often in large numbers. Occurs in fields and hedgerows in summer, many moving into buildings for the winter. Rarely far from human activity.

11

Mole, Hedgehog and Shrews

▼ Hedgehog *Erinaceus europaeus* 22–27cm. Easily distinguished by numerous black-tipped spines. Rarely seen before nightfall unless ill.

▲ Mole *Talpa europaea* Body 11–16cm, tail 3cm. Small eyes. Clawed, spade-like front feet. Dense velvety fur. Lives underground for most of the time.

▼ Water Shrew *Neomys fodiens* Body 7–9cm, tail 4–7cm. Fur is velvety, underparts usually white, upper parts blue-grey or dark brown. Near water.

▼ White-toothed Shrew *Crocidura russula* Body 6–9cm, tail 4cm. Teeth have no red tips like most other shrews. Woods, fields and gardens. Not in Britain.

◄ Pygmy Shrew *Sorex minutus* Body 5–6cm, tail 3–5cm. Tail long, at least two-thirds the body. Dark brown above, whitish below. Teeth have red tips.

► Common Shrew *Sorex araneus* Body 6–7cm, tail 3–5cm. Snout long, teeth red-tipped. Dark brown above, yellowish flanks, whitish beneath. Can often be heard squeaking.

Meat-eaters

▶ **Fox** *Vulpes vulpes* Body 60–80cm, tail 30–48cm. Leaves distinctive scent. Tracks dog-like, but pads oval. Male barks, female (vixen) screams. Digs a burrow (earth) or lives in badgers' sets. Largely nocturnal. Occurs throughout Britain and has become common in town suburbs.

◀ **Badger** *Meles meles* Body 67–80cm, tail 12–18cm. Not often seen in daylight except at sunset. Shuffles with body moving from side to side. Tracks show 5 oval pads with main central pad long and oval. A powerful animal, but eats mainly worms and plant food. Many badgers may live in one set – underground tunnels with several entrances. Copses and deciduous woods.

▶ **Otter** *Lutra lutra* Body 62–83cm, tail 35–55cm. Long body with powerful thick tail used for swimming. Broad flat head with small ears. Legs short with webbed feet. Webs can often be seen in the tracks together with the tail marks. Dense under fur prevents the body from getting wet. Eats fish. Mainly nocturnal. Usually near rivers or coasts.

Meat-eaters

▶ **Stoat** *Mustela erminea*
Body 22–29cm, tail 8–12cm.
Long bodied and sinuous,
with short legs. Foxy-red
above with distinct line
separating the white
underparts. In north, turns
white all over in winter except
for black tail tip (and is then
known as ermine). Feeds on
rabbits, voles, birds. Kills by
bite at back of neck. In and
around woods and
hedgerows.

Winter

▶ **Weasel** *Mustela nivalis* Body 17–
23cm, tail 4–7cm. Smaller than stoat
with shorter and less bushy tail which
has no black tip. Long body, sinuous,
with short legs. Head is narrower and
the line separating the upper parts from
the underparts is not as straight as in
the stoat. Often has brown spots on
underparts. Kills by bite at back of neck,
feeding on birds, mice, rats and voles.
Found in woodlands, farmland and
open country.

▶ **Pine Marten** *Martes martes*
Body 43–50cm, tail 20–26cm. A cat-sized animal with a long body, longer legs than a stoat and a long bushy tail used in climbing trees, like the squirrel. Ears large and rounded, pointed snout. Colour is rich brown with yellowish throat patch. Male larger than female. Found in woodland and also more open areas. Beech marten *Martes foina* similar but with white throat patch (not found in Britain).

◀ **Polecat** *Mustela putorius* Body 30–45cm, tail 12–18cm. Like a large stoat with dark brown or black fur with a purplish shine. Lighter on flanks, no white underneath. Face has whitish patches on nose and behind eye. Glands near tail produce a pungent smell. Woods and thickets.

◀ **Wild Cat** *Felis silvestris* Body 48–75cm, tail 25–35cm. The true wild cat is like a large domestic tabby cat with a pattern of bold tiger-like stripes. Head broader, tail thick, short and bushy with black rings and black tip. Hind-quarters more powerful than domestic cat. Wild cat will breed with domestic cat so that a range of types may be found. British ones occur in Scotland only.

15

Deer and other Hooved Animals

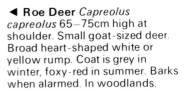

◀ **Roe Deer** *Capreolus capreolus* 65–75cm high at shoulder. Small goat-sized deer. Broad heart-shaped white or yellow rump. Coat is grey in winter, foxy-red in summer. Barks when alarmed. In woodlands.

▶ **Red Deer** *Cervus elaphus* 120–150cm high at shoulder. Large deer, rump patch yellowish-white, tail short. Coat reddish-brown in summer, greyish in winter. Usually in herds. Mainly moorlands in Britain, woodland elsewhere.

◀ **Fallow Deer** *Dama dama* 85–110cm high at shoulder. Tail with black upperside, contrasting with white rump which has black border. Summer coat is orange-brown with white spots, greyer in winter. Usually in herds. Woodland and parks.

▶ **Sika Deer** *Cervus nippon* 80–85cm high at shoulder. No black on upperside of tail so whole rump appears white with black upper border. Male (stag) whistles in mating season to attract females (hinds). Coat is red-brown spotted in summer, grey in winter. Woods. Not common in Britain.

► **Elk** *Alces alces* 150–210cm high at shoulder. Long, heavy, down curved nose. Humped shoulders. Antlers sharp and flat with many sharp points. Coat grey-brown or blackish. Flap of skin on throat. Open woodland with lakes and swamps. Not in Britain.

◄ **Wild Boar** *Sus scrofa* Body 110–150cm, tail 15–20cm. Only pig-like wild mammal in Europe. Male (boar) has large tusks and is solitary. Females (sows) usually in herds. Woods. Not in Britain.

◄ **Wild Goat** *Capra hircus* 65–85cm high at shoulder. Small and shaggy compared to domestic goat. Various colours. Both sexes horned. Hilly areas.

► **Mouflon** *Ovis musimon* 65–75cm high at shoulder. Like small sheep with semi-circular curving horns, smaller or absent in female. Coat hairy, reddish-brown in summer, darker in winter with white patch on sides. Hilly areas. Not in Britain.

Bats

▶ **Pipistrelle** *Pipistrellus pipistrellus* Body 3—5cm, wingspan 19—25cm. Brown or black, with jerky, fast flight. Smallest and commonest European bat.

◀ **Natterer's Bat** *Myotis nattereri* Body 4—5cm, wingspan 25—30cm. Brown above, white below, looking pale in flight. Long rounded ears.

▼ **Daubenton's Bat** *Myotis daubentoni* Body 4—5cm, wingspan 23—27cm. Ears short, pointed tips. Usually flies over water, early in the evening.

◀ **Greater Horseshoe Bat** *Rhinolophus ferrum-equinum* Body 6—7cm, wingspan 34—39cm. Nose has horseshoe-like folds. Flies low over ground.

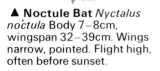

▲ **Noctule Bat** *Nyctalus noctula* Body 7—8cm, wingspan 32—39cm. Wings narrow, pointed. Flight high, often before sunset.

▲ **Long-eared Bat** *Plecotus auritus* Body 4—5cm, wingspan 23—28cm. Large, long, rabbit-shaped ears are distinctive

◀ **Whiskered Bat** *Myotis mystacinus* Body 3—5cm, wingspan 21—24cm. Small bat with narrow wings. Flight fluttering, usually near trees, early in evening.

Seals, Porpoise and Dolphin

▶ Common Seal
Phoca vitulina 130–
160cm. Head puppy-
like, small with short
snout. Body grey or
brown with spots.
Usually seen
swimming, or lying on
sand or mud banks. The
commonest seal in most
parts of NW Europe,
found mainly in
sheltered bays and
estuaries.

◀ Grey Seal *Halichoerus grypus*
195–330cm. Snout long. Body
colour black, fawn or grey with
large spots. Male much larger,
darker, with thick neck. Usually
seen swimming, or lying on rocks.
Locally common, especially on
rocky coasts.

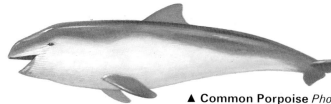

▲ Common Porpoise *Phocoena*
phocoena Up to 200cm. Swims in
'schools', rounded back shows above
water. Single fin is triangular. Head
short, snout blunt. Colour black, white
below. All coasts round Britain.

▼ Common Dolphin *Delphinus*
delphis 150–250cm. Swims in
'schools', fast moving, often leaping
clear of water. Single fin points and
curves towards tail. Head with distinct
forehead.

Birds

Crest
Nape
Back
Wing
Rump
Tail
Legs
Feet

Forehead
Beak or bill
Chin or bib
Throat
Neck
Breast
Side
Wingbars
Flank

♂ **Chaffinch**

Birds are distinguished from all other animals by the possession of feathers. Their front limbs are in the form of wings, and most birds can fly. A bird is structured in such a way that it can do this as efficiently as possible. The wing feathers are shaped so that maximum use can be made of air currents and the bones are honeycombed with spaces full of air to make them light. Feathers are replaced by moulting and kept in good condition by preening, using the beak and oil from special glands.

About 270 kinds of birds live in Europe throughout the year, but many others fly from Africa for the summer, and some fly from the Arctic to spend the winter in Europe. In the following pages, the terms resident or visitor apply only to Britain.

Birds are divided into families and orders for classification, depending on their structure. Measurements are from head to tail.

Crow
all-purpose

Bullfinch
seed-eater

Wren
insect-eater

Curlew
probing mud

◀ In some species of bird, the males are brightly coloured, like this male redstart; the females dull. The symbols used here denote male (♂) and female (♀)

Summer   Winter

◀ Look out for the labels Summer and Winter which tell you whether an illustration is of a bird's summer or winter plumage. Here is a dotterel at different times of the year.

Young   Adult

◀ Young birds such as the robin often have different patterns and colours, especially when the adults are brightly coloured. Gulls take 2 to 3 years for the young to develop their adult plumage.

CLUES AND HINTS

Watching: When studying birds, spend a lot of time just watching. Only then will you learn their shape, behaviour and song, so that eventually a bird can be identified almost without thinking – a magpie hopping and jerking its long tail or the flash of white rump as a bullfinch slips into the bushes. A good pair of binoculars is important. Be quiet and patient. Never disturb nesting birds.

Song: Birdsong is an invaluable aid in identifying a bird. Learn songs and calls through recordings, as well as by listening with more experienced people.
Identification: Always make notes on the spot when you have seen a bird. As far as possible, it should be compared with something familiar and all details jotted down before consulting an identification guide.

Barn owl tearing flesh

Kingfisher fish-eater

◀ Different parts of a bird's body are adapted to the way it lives. Beaks show the greatest diversity, though birds in the same family have similar beak shapes. The shapes are adapted to the kind of food the bird eats and the way it gets its food.

21

Shearwater, Fulmar, Gannet, Diver and Grebes

▶ **Fulmar** *Fulmarus glacialis* 46cm. Gull-like, wings long, straight and stiff in flight. No black tips. Bill thick, short with tube-like nostrils. Nests on sea cliffs. Resident.

◀ **Manx Shearwater** *Puffinus puffinus* 36cm. Flies low over water, wings held stiffly. Nests in burrows on coast. Resident.

▼ **Great Crested Grebe** *Podiceps cristatus* 46cm. Summer: ear tufts and ruff. Winter: long white neck, white patch by eye. Breeds lakes and rivers. Often on coast. Resident.

Summer

Winter

▲ **Gannet** *Sula bassana* 91cm. Large white bird, pointed long wings, black tips. Long sharp bill. Resident.

▶ **Black-throated Diver** *Gavia arctica* 63cm. Breeds in Scotland. Resident and winter visitor on coasts.

Summer

Winter

▼ **Little Grebe** *Tachybaptus ruficollis* 25cm. Small, dumpy grebe, diving often. Freshwater. Common. Summer: chestnut cheeks and neck. Winter: brown back. Resident.

Winter

Summer

Cormorants, Heron, Bittern and Stork

Continental form

Atlantic form

▶ **Shag** *Phalacrocorax aristotelis* 76cm. Like small cormorant, but all black, no white patches. Both sexes have small crest in summer. Breeds sea cliffs, not seen inland. Resident.

▶ **Bittern** *Botaurus stellaris* 76cm. Seldom seen. Distinctive 'booming' call in summer. Stands motionless at edge of reed beds, often bill pointing upwards. Breeds in reed beds. Resident and visitor.

▲ **Cormorant** *Phalacrocorax carbo* 91cm. Large black bird, long neck and hooked bill. Breeds sea cliffs, sometimes seen inland. Resident.

◀ **Heron** *Ardea cinerea* 91cm. Very large grey bird with long neck, legs and bill. Broad wings, trailing legs and neck folded back in flight, with slow, flapping wing beats. Resident.

▶ **White Stork** *Ciconia ciconia* 102cm. Very large white bird with red legs and bill. Wings with black edges. Nests on or near houses. Not in Britain.

Ducks

◀ **Mallard** *Anas platyrhynchos* 58cm. Male has green head, chestnut breast. Female brown with blue/purple speculum; the male is similar when it moults (August). Large numbers on coast in winter. Common. Resident.

▶ **Teal** *Anas crecca* 36cm. Small, agile duck. Male has chestnut head, green eye patch. Back and sides grey, long white stripe down side. Female brown, speculum green. Male call, a musical whistle. Flight rapid. Flocks in winter. Upends when feeding. Resident.

◀ **Wigeon** *Anas penelope* 46cm. Male has chestnut head with creamy-white centre. White line on side, black and white near tail. Female brown, bill blue. Male call is double whistle. Winter visitor to coast and lakes.

▶ ▼ **Pintail** *Anas acuta* 63cm. Male has long pointed tail, brown head, long white neck with white 'finger' behind eye. Black and white near tail. Female brown, shorter, pointed tail, long neck, blue-grey bill. A few breed but mainly winter visitor in small numbers.

▲ Shoveler *Anas clypeata* 51cm. Both sexes have large, heavy, spoon-shaped bill and low forehead. Dabbles for food on lakes and ponds. Resident and winter visitor.

▼ Tufted Duck *Aythya fuligula* 43cm. Male is black with white sides and tuft at back of head. Female dark brown, paler sides, small tuft. Feeds by diving. Resident and winter visitor.

◄ Pochard *Aythya ferina* 46cm. Male has red head, black breast. Female brown, blue band on bill. Dives to feed. Resident and winter visitor.

► Goldeneye *Bucephala clangula* 46cm. Male is mainly white. Head rounded, greenish-black with white patch by bill. Female has brown head, white collar, grey body. Winter visitor to coasts.

◄ Common Scoter *Melanitta nigra* 51cm. Male is black with rounded back and heavy head. Bill yellow with large knob at base. Female brown, pale cheeks and neck. Winter visitor to coasts.

25

Ducks

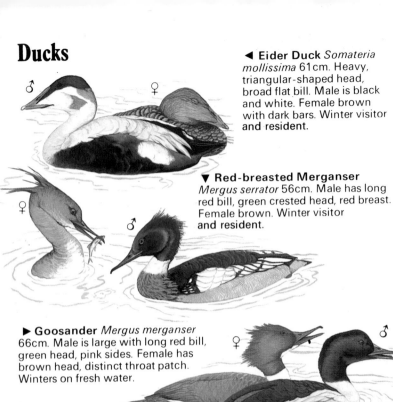

◄ **Eider Duck** *Somateria mollissima* 61cm. Heavy, triangular-shaped head, broad flat bill. Male is black and white. Female brown with dark bars. Winter visitor and resident.

▼ **Red-breasted Merganser** *Mergus serrator* 56cm. Male has long red bill, green crested head, red breast. Female brown. Winter visitor and resident.

► **Goosander** *Mergus merganser* 66cm. Male is large with long red bill, green head, pink sides. Female has brown head, distinct throat patch. Winters on fresh water.

◄ **Smew** *Mergus albellus* 41cm. Male is dumpy, black and white with crest and slender bill. Female has chestnut head, white cheeks. Lakes and rivers, sometimes coasts. Winter visitor.

► **Shelduck** *Tadorna tadorna* 61cm. Male and female similar, but male has knob on red bill. Flight slower than other ducks. Breeds on coasts. Resident.

Geese and Swans

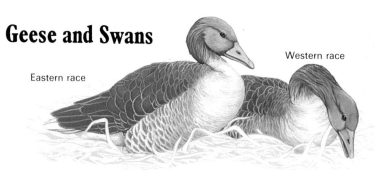

Eastern race

Western race

▼ Pink-footed Goose
Anser brachyrhynchus 68cm.
Head and neck dark. Bill and
feet pink. Winter visitor to
coasts.

▲ Greylag *Anser anser* 84cm. Heavy
orange or pink bill. Grey
forewings. Calls like
domestic goose. Winter
visitor.

Dark-bellied form

Light-bellied
form

▶ Brent Goose *Branta
bernicla* 58cm. Small dark
goose, black head, neck and
breast. Belly dark or white.
Barnacle goose *B. leucopsis*
similar, but larger and head
white. Winter visitor to coasts.

◀ Canada Goose *Branta
canadensis* 97cm. Large
goose with black head and
neck. White throat patch.
Introduced from North
America. Resident.

▼ Whooper Swan
Cygnus cygnus 152cm.
Bill yellow, neck
straight. 'Whooping'
call-note. Coastal and
inland waters. Winter
visitor.

▼ Mute Swan
Cygnus olor 152cm.
Large white bird. Bill
red with black knob.
Neck usually curved.
Resident on lakes and
rivers.

Birds of Prey

Light form

Dark form

◀ **Buzzard** *Buteo buteo* 53cm. Both sexes various shades of brown. Barred tail. Circles with little wing flapping. Resident.

▶ **Golden Eagle** *Aquila chrysaetos* 84cm. Both sexes brown, adult has golden head. Tail square. Heavy head visible in flight. Resident in mountains of northern Britain.

◀ **Goshawk** *Accipiter gentilis* 53cm. Rounded wings, barred underparts, long tail. Female larger than male. Flies fast and low when hunting. Few breed in woodland. Resident.

▼ **Sparrowhawk** *Accipiter nisus* 33cm. Male grey above, barred reddish breast. Female larger, brown, barred breast. Flight fast and low when hunting. Woodland. Common. Resident.

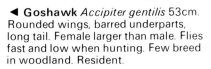

♀ ♂

▼ **Marsh Harrier** *Circus aeruginosus* 51cm. Large hawk with broad wings seen flying low over marshes. Male has long grey tail and wings. Female dark with pale head and throat.

▼ **Hen Harrier** *Circus cyaneus* 46cm. Male is grey above, long narrow wings, long tail. Female brown, white rump. Moorland, often on coast in winter.

♀ ♂ ♀

♀ ♂

▲ **Hobby** *Falco subbuteo* 33cm. Sexes similar. Dashing, swift-like flight. Summer visitor.

▼ **Osprey** *Pandion haliaetus* 56cm. Sexes similar. Black line through eye. Breeds Scotland near fresh water. Summer visitor.

▲ **Peregrine** *Falco peregrinus* 43cm. Sexes similar. Flight rapid and dashing. Breeds on coastal and mountain cliffs. Resident.

◄ **Merlin** *Falco columbarius* 30cm. Small falcon. Male has grey-blue back, reddish breast with brown streaks. Female brown, streaked breast. Flight swift, few quick wing beats followed by glide. Not common. Resident.

► **Kestrel** *Falco tinnunculus* 33cm. Long pointed wings, long tail. Usually seen hovering, especially near motorways. Male has chestnut back with black spots, black tail bar. Female brown, barred back and tail. Common. Resident.

Game Birds

▶ **Red Grouse** *Lagopus lagopus scoticus* 38cm. Both sexes red-brown, darker wings and tail. Red wattle over eye. Wings down, curved when gliding. Breeds moorland. Resident.

▼ **Willow Grouse** *Lagopus lagopus* 38cm. Similar to ptarmigan but at lower altitudes. Male has brown back in summer. Female as ptarmigan. Turns white in winter, no black on head. Not in Britain.

♂ Winter ♀ Winter

♀ Summer ♂ Summer

▲ **Black Grouse** *Tetrao tetrix* 53cm. Male is blue-black with red wattles, curved, forked tail. Female brown, barred feathers. Breeds moorland. Resident.

▼ **Capercaillie** *Tetrao urogallus* 86cm. Turkey-sized game bird. Male dark grey, red wattles. Female brown, barred feathers. Woodlands in Scotland. Resident.

▼ **Ptarmigan** *Lagopus mutus* 36cm. Summer: white wings, male body grey, female brown. Winter: all white. Mountains of Scotland. Resident.

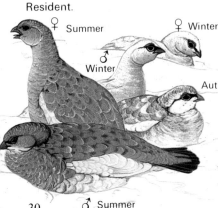

♀ Summer ♀ Winter

♂ Winter

Autumn

♂

♀

♂ Summer

► **Hazel Grouse** *Bonasa bonasia* 36cm. Small brown game bird. Both sexes have round, grey tail with black band. Short crest on head. Male has black throat, white border. Not in Britain.

▲ **Quail** *Coturnix coturnix* 18cm. Very small, dumpy game bird. Sandy-brown with darker streaks. Shy, but can be heard calling in grass or corn. Summer visitor.

► **Partridge** *Perdix perdix* 30cm. Round, dumpy, brown game bird with chestnut head, reddish tail, grey neck. Male chestnut, horseshoe-shaped mark on breast, paler or absent in females. Farmland. Resident.

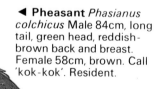

◄ **Pheasant** *Phasianus colchicus* Male 84cm, long tail, green head, reddish-brown back and breast. Female 58cm, brown. Call 'kok-kok'. Resident.

31

Crane, Rails and Crakes

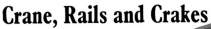

▼ Moorhen *Gallinula chloropus*
33cm. Red forehead and bill,
brown back, dark-blue breast,
white stripe along side, white
patch by tail. Near water. Resident.

▼ Crane *Grus grus*
114cm. Large heron-
like bird. Long neck and
legs. Head and neck
black with long white
stripe, body grey. Long
black, drooping 'tail'
feathers. Not in Britain.

▲ Coot *Fulica atra* 38cm. Both sexes
black with broad white forehead. Back
rounded. Large ponds and lakes.
Resident.

▲ Spotted Crake
Porzana porzana 23cm.
Small brown bird,
streaked and spotted
with white, barred
sides. Jerks tail when
anxious. Swamps and
wet places. Winter
visitor.

▲ Water Rail *Rallus
aquaticus* 28cm. Long,
slender, red bill with
black tip. Black and
white barred flanks.
Resident.

► Corncrake *Crex
crex* 25cm. Small
thrush-sized brown
bird, chestnut on wings.
Summer visitor.

Waders

◄ Oystercatcher
Haematopus ostralegus
43cm. Long orange bill,
pinkish legs. Breeds coasts
and estuaries. Sometimes
inland. Resident.

▼ Golden Plover *Pluvialis
apricaria* 28cm In summer,
back spangled black and gold.
Breeds moorland. Note liquid
whistle. Resident

Southern form
Summer

Northern form
Summer

Winter

▼ Ringed Plover *Charadrius
hiaticula* 19cm. Resident. **Little
Ringed Plover** *Charadrius dubius*
15cm. Small, active birds, pointed
wings. Inland. Summer visitor.

Little ringed plover

Ringed plover

► Dotterel *Eudromias
morinellus* 23cm. Summer: white
eye stripe, white band dividing
chestnut belly from grey breast.
Winter: underparts duller. No wing
bar in flight. Summer visitor.

Winter

Summer

◄ Lapwing *Vanellus
vanellus* 30cm. Long
crest. Calls 'pee wit'.
Breeds moors, fields.
Resident.

Winter

Summer

▲ Turnstone *Arenaria interpres*
23cm. Patchy appearance in summer,
orange legs. Rocky shores. Winter
visitor.

Waders

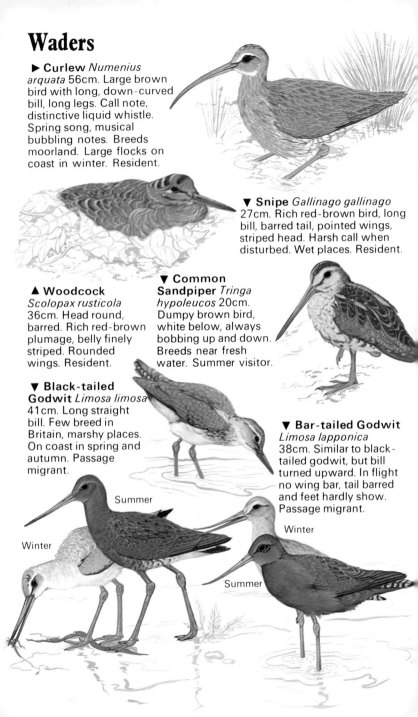

▶ **Curlew** *Numenius arquata* 56cm. Large brown bird with long, down-curved bill, long legs. Call note, distinctive liquid whistle. Spring song, musical bubbling notes. Breeds moorland. Large flocks on coast in winter. Resident.

▼ **Snipe** *Gallinago gallinago* 27cm. Rich red-brown bird, long bill, barred tail, pointed wings, striped head. Harsh call when disturbed. Wet places. Resident.

▲ **Woodcock** *Scolopax rusticola* 36cm. Head round, barred. Rich red-brown plumage, belly finely striped. Rounded wings. Resident.

▼ **Common Sandpiper** *Tringa hypoleucos* 20cm. Dumpy brown bird, white below, always bobbing up and down. Breeds near fresh water. Summer visitor.

▼ **Black-tailed Godwit** *Limosa limosa* 41cm. Long straight bill. Few breed in Britain, marshy places. On coast in spring and autumn. Passage migrant.

▼ **Bar-tailed Godwit** *Limosa lapponica* 38cm. Similar to black-tailed godwit, but bill turned upward. In flight no wing bar, tail barred and feet hardly show. Passage migrant.

Summer

Winter

Winter

Summer

◄ **Redshank** *Tringa totanus* 28cm. Long red legs and bill. Distinctive liquid call of 3 notes. Flight rapid. Breeds marshy areas, inland and coast. Resident.

▼ **Greenshank** *Tringa nebularia* 30cm. Upturned bill. Greenish legs. Dark grey-brown upper parts, white underparts. Head, neck and breast spotted. Breeds moorland near water in Scotland. Seen as migrant on coasts in spring and autumn.

Winter

Summer

◄ **Dunlin** *Calidris alpina* 18cm. Small dumpy wader. Flocks along tide edge in winter. Breeds moorland, marshes. Resident.

Summer

Winter

Winter

◄ **Curlew Sandpiper** *Calidris ferruginea* 19cm. Like dunlin, bill more downcurved. Often with dunlin on seashore. Migrant spring and autumn.

Summer

▲ **Knot** *Calidris canutus* 25cm. Bill short, thick and straight. Neck short, rounded body. Large flocks on coasts. Winter visitor.

► **Sanderling** *Calidris alba* 20cm. Summer: rich brown upper parts, white below. Winter: very pale with black patch showing in front of wing. Bill short. Seen on tide line feeding with other waders. Winter visitor.

Summer

Winter

Waders

◀ **Avocet** *Recurvirostra avosetta*
43cm. Long thin, upturned bill. Black
and white plumage, long slate-blue
legs. Shows black and white pattern in
flight. Feeds by moving head from side
to side in shallow water. Summer
visitor, migrant.

▼ **Ruff** *Philomachus pugnax*
30cm. Male is unmistakable in
summer – large ruff of feathers on
neck which varies in colour.
Passage migrant in spring and
autumn.

♂ Winter   ♀   ♂ Summer

♂ Summer

▲ **Black-winged Stilt**
Himantopus himantopus 38cm.
Very long red legs, straight black
bill. Male has black back with
white underparts. Female similar
but with no black on head. In
flight, dark pointed wings
contrast with white body. Rare
summer visitor.

♀   ♂ Winter

◀ **Stone Curlew** *Burhinus
oedicnemus* 41cm. Bill short, gull-
like. Large yellow eye. Rounded
head. Colour sandy-brown with
darker streaks. Heathland, open
woodland. Summer visitor.

Gulls

▶ **Black-headed Gull**
Larus ridibundus 38cm.
Small gull. Inland and
coasts. Nests in
colonies. The similar
Mediterranean gull *L.
melanocephalus* has no
black on wing. The little
gull *L. minutus* is very
small. Resident.

Mediterranean
gull in winter

Little gull
in winter

Black-headed gull
in winter

▼ **Lesser Black-backed
Gull** *Larus fuscus* 53cm. Bill
yellow, red spot. Legs yellow,
slate-grey upper parts. Wing
has black tips, spotted white.
Nests at seashore. Resident.

British
form

Scandinavian form

▼ **Great Black-
backed Gull** *Larus
marinus* 68cm. The
largest gull. Legs pink.
Bill heavy, yellow with
red spot. Chiefly on
coasts but also inland.
Resident.

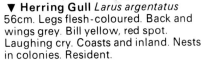

▼ **Herring Gull** *Larus argentatus*
56cm. Legs flesh-coloured. Back and
wings grey. Bill yellow, red spot.
Laughing cry. Coasts and inland. Nests
in colonies. Resident.

◀ **Common Gull**
Larus canus 41cm. Legs
and bill greenish yellow.
Back and wings grey,
wing tips black with
white spots. Often
inland as well as on
coast. Resident.

Gulls and Terns

▶ **Kittiwake** *Rissa tridactyla*
41cm. Yellow bill (no marks).
Dark legs, dove-grey back.
Wing tips black, no white spots.
Call 'kit-i-wake'. Nests in
colonies. Resident.

◀ **Black Tern** *Chlidonias niger*
24cm. Bill black, legs red, white
under tail, pointed wings. Tail
forked. Flight is butterfly-like over
reeds and marshes. Passage
migrant.

▶ **Common Tern** *Sterna hirundo*
36cm. Long pointed wings,
forked tail, red bill with black tip.
Head black, back grey. Flight
bouncy, often diving into sea to
fish. Harsh single call note.
Coasts. Also inland. Summer
visitor.

▶ **Sandwich Tern**
Sterna sandvicensis
41cm. Large tern.
Heavy black bill with
yellow tip. Forked tail.
Black head, feathers
forming crest at back.
Legs black. Harsh
rasping call distinctive.
Coastal. Summer
visitor.

◀ **Little Tern** *Sterna albifrons*
24cm. Smallest tern. Yellow bill
with black tip, legs yellow. Tail
forked. Sandy coasts and shingle.
Summer visitor.

Auks

◀ **Guillemot** *Uria aalge* 41cm. Bill straight, slender, long. Neck slender. White line on wing. Flight whirring on small, narrow, rapidly beating wings. Low over water. Nests in colonies on sea cliffs. Resident.

Summer

Winter

Summer

▶ **Puffin** *Fratercula arctica* 30cm. Small auk with large beak, flattened sideways. In summer brightly coloured, red, blue and yellow; less noticeable in winter. Legs orange. Nests in burrows on coasts and islands. Carries many fish at a time in beak. Resident.

Winter

Summer

◀ **Razorbill** *Alca torda* 41cm. Very like guillemot but bill short, deep and heavy looking, with white mark across it. Nests in colonies on sea cliffs with guillemots. Resident.

Winter

Pigeon, Doves and Cuckoo

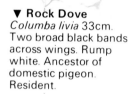

► Stock Dove
Columba oenas 33cm.
Like small woodpigeon.
No white on wings or
neck. Two narrow
black wingbars. Rump
grey. Woodland.
Resident.

◄ Woodpigeon
Columba palumbus
41cm. Largest pigeon.
White on neck and
broad white mark on
wings. Resident.

▼ Rock Dove
Columba livia 33cm.
Two broad black bands
across wings. Rump
white. Ancestor of
domestic pigeon.
Resident.

◄ Turtle Dove
Streptopelia turtur
28cm. Slender pigeon
with rounded tail.
Fields, small woods.
Summer visitor.

◄ Collared Dove
Streptopelia decaocto
30cm. Slender, buff-
coloured dove, distinct
black patch on neck.
Towns and villages.
Resident.

► Cuckoo *Cuculus canorus*
33cm. Male call is well-
known 'cuckoo'. Blue-grey
back, barred breast. Female
brown, lays single egg in nests
of other birds. Rare. Young
cuckoo ejects young and is
reared by its foster parents.
Summer visitor.

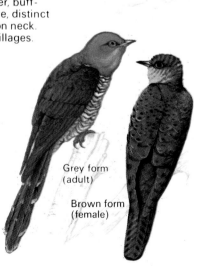

Grey form
(adult)

Brown form
(female)

Owls

Light-breasted form

Dark-breasted form

► **Barn Owl** *Tyto alba* 36cm. Long rounded wings, large round head. Upper parts golden brown with black spots. Flies silently at dusk. Near buildings. Resident.

◄ **Eagle Owl** *Bubo bubo* 68cm. Very large owl. Long ear tufts, large orange eyes. Brown with boldly streaked breast. Not in Britain.

▼ **Pygmy Owl** *Glaucidium passerinum* 18cm. Small owl. Active by day. Not in Britain.

Brown form   Grey form

► **Little Owl** *Athene noctua* 23cm. Broad head with yellow eyes. Brown back with large white spots. Active by day. Open country. Resident.

◄ **Tawny Owl** *Strix aluco* 38cm. Brown or grey-brown owl with heavily streaked plumage. Large head and black eyes, no ear tufts. Active at night. Voice is the familiar hoot. Wooded areas. Resident.

◄ **Long-eared Owl** *Asio otus* 36cm. Long ear tufts, orange eyes, body slimmer than tawny owl. Colour similar. Active at night. Chiefly in coniferous woods. Resident.

► **Short-eared Owl** *Asio flammeus* 38cm. Hunts by day. Usually seen flying low, on long wings. Moors, open country. Resident.

41

Nightjar, Swift, Kingfisher and Related Birds

► **Nightjar** *Caprimulgus europaeus* 28cm. Moth-like flight at dusk. Long wings and tail. Open woods. Summer visitor.

♂
♀

◄ **Swift** *Apus apus* 16cm. Usually seen in flight. Dark with long, curved, pointed wings which flicker rapidly. Tail forked. Screams in flight, especially in the evening. Summer visitor.

◄ **Kingfisher** *Alcedo atthis* 16cm. Brightly-coloured bird with large head, long pointed bill. Flies low and very fast. Fresh water. Resident.

▼ **Roller** *Coracias garrulus* 30cm. Like small jay in size. Chestnut back, blue-green underparts unmistakable both in flight and on ground. Not in Britain.

Crest up

Crest down

▲ **Bee-eater** *Merops apiaster* 28cm. Curved bill, brilliant colours. Rare summer visitor.

► **Hoopoe** *Upupa epops* 28cm. Long crest, tipped with black, long curved bill. Buff-pink head and breast. Rare visitor to Britain.

Woodpeckers

► **Black Woodpecker**
Dryocopus martius 46cm. All
black woodpecker with
crimson crown, yellow eyes
and pale yellow bill. Large
bird. Coniferous forest, not
Britain.

▼ **Wryneck** *Jynx torquilla*
16cm. Not often seen. Grey-
brown with upper parts
mottled and streaked,
underparts barred. Small bill,
tail barred. Summer visitor.

► **Grey-headed
Woodpecker** *Picus canus*
25cm. Similar to green
woodpecker but smaller with
grey head and neck. Not in
Britain.

► **Green Woodpecker**
Picus viridis 30cm. Large,
jackdaw-sized woodpecker.
Dark green upper parts, red
crown, yellow rump. Often
heard, when laughing cry
is easily recognized.
Flight up and down, with
wings closing every few
beats; long bill, short tail
noticeable. Often feeds on
ground. Deciduous woodland
with old trees. Resident.

Woodpeckers

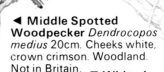

▶ Great Spotted Woodpecker
Dendrocopos major
23cm. Black and white with black crown and crimson underneath tail. Male has crimson patch on head. All kinds of woodland. Resident.

◀ Middle Spotted Woodpecker *Dendrocopos medius* 20cm. Cheeks white, crown crimson. Woodland. Not in Britain.

▼ White-backed Woodpecker *Dendrocopos leucotos* 25cm. Similar in colour to great spotted woodpecker but no black on crown. Lower back white. Not in Britain.

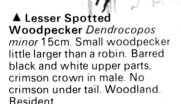

▲ Lesser Spotted Woodpecker *Dendrocopos minor* 15cm. Small woodpecker little larger than a robin. Barred black and white upper parts, crimson crown in male. No crimson under tail. Woodland. Resident.

Larks, Martins and Swallow

► **Skylark** *Alauda arvensis* 18cm. Small crest, long tail with white outer tail feathers. Distinctive continuous song as bird rises and then descends with open wings. Resident

▼ **Woodlark** *Lullula arborea* 15cm. Tail short, distinct white eye stripe meeting at back of head. Open woodland. Resident.

▲ **Crested Lark** *Galerida cristata* 16cm. Distinct, long crest. Buff, not white, outer tail feathers, tail short. Not in Britain.

▼ **House Martin** *Delichon urbica* 13cm. White rump and underparts, upper parts blue. No breast band. Tail short with slight fork. Usually near buildings. Summer visitor.

▼ **Sand Martin** *Riparia riparia* 13cm. White breast has brown band across. Upper parts and wings brown. Usually seen flying near water. Summer visitor.

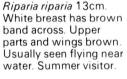

▲ **Swallow** *Hirundo rustica* 19cm. Long tail streamers in adult. Long wings, blue neck-band, red throat with buffish-white underparts, wings pointed. Flight wheeling and circling. Summer visitor.

Crows

◄ **Raven** *Corvus corax*
63cm. The largest crow. All
black, bill heavy, stout. Easily
distinguished by 'croaking'
note. In flight, tail is wedge-
shaped. Often soars and
tumbles in flight. Hills and
coastal cliffs. Resident.

► **Carrion Crow** *Corvus corone
corone* 46cm. Bill thicker and
heavier than rook, no bare patch
at base of bill. Distinctive harsh
call. Usually in pairs. Resident.

◄ **Hooded Crow** *Corvus corone
cornix* 46cm. Like carrion crow, but
has grey back and underparts. Closely
related, often interbreed. Resident.

► **Jackdaw** *Corvus
monedula* 33cm. Small
crow. Grey nape, short
bill. Call 'jack jack'
distinctive. Often with
rooks. Usually in small
groups, even when
nesting. Flies more
rapidly than other
crows. Resident.

◄ **Rook** *Corvus frugilegus* 46cm.
Black crow with bare patch of skin
at base of bill. Feathers at top of
leg loose and 'baggy'. Usually in
flocks, nesting in colonies.
Farmland. Resident.

46

Crows and Oriole

▲ Magpie *Pica pica*
46cm. Distinctive black
and white plumage.
Long wedge-shaped
tail. Usually hops, but
can walk. Chattering
call. Open country with
hedges, open
woodland. Resident.

▲ Jay *Garrulus glandarius* 36cm.
White rump and black tail easily
seen in jerky flight. Bright blue and
black on wings, pinkish-brown
body. Harsh call. Resident.

▶ Chough *Pyrrhocorax
pyrrhocorax* 38cm. Like large
slender jackdaw with bright
red, long, downward-curved
bill and red legs. Flies with
the feathers at tips of rounded
wings well separated, soaring
and diving with ease. Coastal
and inland cliffs. Resident.

♂   ♀

◀ Golden Oriole *Oriolus
oriolus* 24cm. Thrush-sized,
bright yellow body
contrasting with black wings
and tail make male bird
unmistakable. Female and
young greenish-yellow with
dark wings and tail.
Distinctive musical whistle.
Rare summer visitor.

47

Tits

◄ **Blue Tit** *Parus caeruleus* 11cm. White cheeks with line through eye, and bright blue crown. Gardens and woodland. Resident.

▲ **Great Tit** *Parus major* 14cm. The largest tit, underparts yellow with black streak down centre, cheek patches white on black head. Often feeds upside down. Resident.

► **Marsh Tit** *Parus palustris* 11cm. Glossy black cap and black chin on otherwise brown tit, darker above, paler below. Double harsh call note. Woods and copses. Resident.

► **Willow Tit** *Parus montanus* (far right) 11cm. Similar, dull not glossy crown and light patch on side of wing. Damp woodland. Resident.

▲ **Coal Tit** *Parus ater* 11cm. Black head with white patch at back of neck, whitish cheeks, black throat. Double white wingbar. Woodland, especially conifers. Resident.

► **Long-tailed Tit** *Aegithalos caudatus* 14cm. Very long narrow tail. White crown bordered with black. Young birds have no pink on them. Woodland, hedges. Resident.

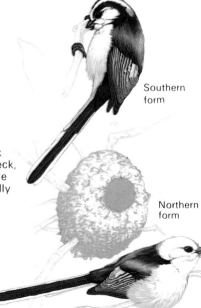

Southern form

Northern form

Parrotbill, Nuthatch, Creeper, Wren and Dipper

▶ **Bearded Reedling**
Panurus biarmicus 16cm. It is
the only species of parrotbill
found in Europe. Both sexes
have long brown tail and
upper parts. Male has black
stripe by bill and grey head,
black under tail. Flight slow,
with trailing tail. Resident.

▶ **Tree Creeper**
Certhia familiaris
14cm. Small brown
bird with curved
bill, white
underparts. Usually
seen 'jerking' up
tree trunk,
supported by tail.
Woodlands.
Resident.

Treecreeper

Short-toed treecreeper
(buff belly)

▲ **Nuthatch** *Sitta europaea* 14cm.
Large head and bill, short tail, slate-
blue upper parts, black line through
eye, buff orange underparts.
Woodlands. Resident.

◀ **Wren** *Troglodytes troglodytes*
10cm. Tiny, stumpy, dark brown with
short, cocked tail. Flight short, with
whirring wings. Woods and gardens.
Resident.

▶ **Dipper** *Cinclus cinclus* 18cm. A
plump, thrush-sized brown bird with a
white throat and short tail. Always by
running water, bobs up and down on
stones. Resident.

Thrushes, Chats and Redstarts

▶ **Song Thrush** *Turdus philomelos*
23cm. Brown bird with buff, spotted
breast. Eye large, dark. Hops, cocking
head to one side. Cracks snails on
stones. Gardens. Resident.

▲ **Redwing** *Turdus iliacus*
20cm. Broad white eye stripe,
red patch on flanks, dark
brown back. Fields. Winter
visitor.

▲ **Mistle Thrush** *Turdus
viscivorus* 28cm. Larger, greyer
bird than song thrush, white tips
to tail feathers, underside of wing
pale in flight. Resident.

▲ **Fieldfare** *Turdus
pilaris* 25cm. Grey head
and chestnut back.
Pale grey rump, black
tail in flight. Winter
visitor.

▶ **Blackbird** *Turdus
merula* 25cm. Male all
black, yellow bill.
Female dark brown.
Chattering call.
Gardens, woods.
Resident.

◀ **Wheatear**
Oenanthe oenanthe
15cm. Both sexes have
white rump, easily seen
in flight. Male is blue-
grey with black tail and
wings. Heaths and
hillsides. Summer
visitor.

▶ **Black Redstart** *Phoenicurus ochruros* 14cm. Both sexes have red rump and tail. Tail flicked constantly Summer visitor and passage migrant.

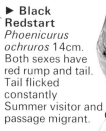

▲ **Nightingale** *Luscinia megarhynchos* 16cm. Shy bird usually discovered by liquid song. All brown, no markings. Woods and thickets. Summer visitor.

▼ **Blue throat** *Luscinia svecica* 14cm. Robin-like with blue throat. Flicks tail. Rare visitor.

▶ **Stonechat** *Saxicola torquata* 13cm. Usually seen on gorse bush or bracken, flicking wings and tail with clicking call. Commons, hillsides. Resident.

♂ White-spotted form

♂ Red-spotted form

▼ **Robin** *Erithacus rubecula* 14cm. Red breast with pale grey border, brown back. Gardens, woodlands. Resident.

▶ **Whinchat** *Saxicola rubetra* 13cm. Both sexes have eye stripe, white in male, buff in female. Moors, heaths. Summer visitor.

▶ **Redstart** *Phoenicurus phoenicurus* 14cm. Both sexes have chestnut tail which is always quivering. Gardens, open woodland, hillsides. Summer visitor.

51

Warblers

▼ **Sedge Warbler** *Acrocephalus schoenobaenus* 13cm. Brown bird, broad white eye stripe and streaked back. Not often seen. Chattering song. Summer visitor.

▲ **Reed Warbler** *Acrocephalus scirpaceus* 13cm. Brown bird, no streaks on back. Reed beds, long grass near water. Summer visitor.

◄ **Blackcap** *Sylvia atricapilla* 14cm. Keeps to tree tops, singing its sweet liquid song. Male grey-brown with black cap. Female brown, with red-brown cap. Resident in southern Britain.

► **Garden Warbler** *Sylvia borin* 14cm. Brown bird, paler below, with no markings. Shy, like blackcap. Song similar but more hurried. Prefers woodland with more undergrowth than blackcap. Summer visitor.

Warblers and Goldcrest

▼ Dartford Warbler
Sylvia undata 13cm.
Dark bird with long
tail, often cocked
upwards. Heaths.
Resident.

▲ Whitethroat *Sylvia
communis* 14cm. White
throat, reddish-brown on
wings, white outer tail
feathers in both sexes. Song,
rapid chatter. Hedges and
thickets. Summer visitor.

▶ Willow Warbler
Phylloscopus trochilus 11cm.
Brownish-yellow warbler, pale
brown legs. Song, descending
liquid notes. Feeds in tree tops.
Summer visitor.

▲ Chiffchaff
Phylloscopus collybita
11cm. Brownish-
yellow warbler with
black legs. Song
'chiffchaff' repeated.
Woodland. Summer
visitor.

▼ Wood Warbler
Phylloscopus sibilatrix
13cm. Yellow breast
and eye stripe.
Woodland. Summer
visitor.

◀ Goldcrest *Regulus regulus* 9cm.
Very small, plump, greenish bird with
white wingbars and gold crown
between black stripes. Woodland.
Resident.

53

Flycatchers, Dunnock and Pipits

◀ **Pied Flycatcher** *Ficedula hypoleuca* 13cm. White wing patch, white on side of tail. Catches insects. Summer visitor.

♀

▶ **Spotted Flycatcher** *Muscicapa striata* 14cm. Makes short flights to catch insects. Summer visitor.

♂ Summer

▶ **Dunnock** *Prunella modularis* 15cm. Often seen creeping mouse-like through undergrowth. Robin-like, but grey breast. Brown, streaked back. Resident.

▼ **Meadow Pipit** *Anthus pratensis* 15cm. Like small, slender skylark, no crest. Open country and moorland. Resident.

▶ **Tree Pipit** *Anthus trivialis* 15cm. Very similar to meadow pipit but warmer brown. Distinctive song, delivered on outstretched wings, trills followed by single notes. Open woodland. Summer visitor.

▶ **Rock Pipit** *Anthus spinoletta* 16cm. Much darker brown than meadow pipit, with dark legs and greyish, not white, outer tail feathers. Usually found on rocky sea shores. Resident.

Wagtails, Waxwing, Shrikes and Starling

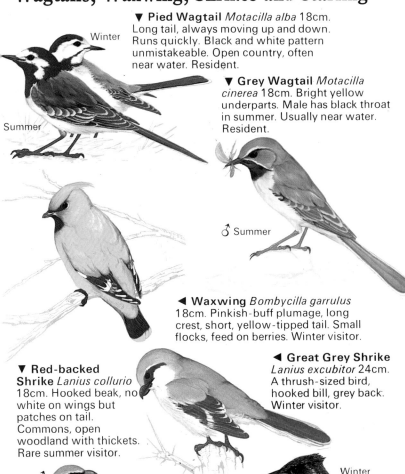

▼ **Pied Wagtail** *Motacilla alba* 18cm. Long tail, always moving up and down. Runs quickly. Black and white pattern unmistakeable. Open country, often near water. Resident.

Winter

Summer

▼ **Grey Wagtail** *Motacilla cinerea* 18cm. Bright yellow underparts. Male has black throat in summer. Usually near water. Resident.

♂ Summer

◄ **Waxwing** *Bombycilla garrulus* 18cm. Pinkish-buff plumage, long crest, short, yellow-tipped tail. Small flocks, feed on berries. Winter visitor.

◄ **Great Grey Shrike** *Lanius excubitor* 24cm. A thrush-sized bird, hooked bill, grey back. Winter visitor.

▼ **Red-backed Shrike** *Lanius collurio* 18cm. Hooked beak, no white on wings but patches on tail. Commons, open woodland with thickets. Rare summer visitor.

♂

♀

Winter

▶ **Starling** *Sturnus vulgaris* 21cm. Long pointed bill, yellow in summer. Short tail, glossy black feathers, speckled in winter. Resident.

Summer

55

Finches

◄ Greenfinch *Carduelis chloris*
15cm. Flight up and down showing
pattern of yellow and green. Gardens,
open areas. Resident.

▼ Hawfinch *Coccothraustes
coccothraustes* 18cm. Large finch
with thick bill. Short tail, broad white
patches on wings. Call note, a metallic
click. Woodland. Resident.

► Goldfinch
Carduelis carduelis
13cm. Black and
yellow pattern with red
on head. Flight erratic,
often calling all the
time. Resident.

▼ Linnet *Acanthis
cannabina* 13cm.
Streaked, chestnut
back, black and white
tail feathers, head
streaked greyish.
Twitters. Resident.

▼ Siskin *Carduelis
spinus* 12cm. Small
finch, short forked tail.
Yellow rump, wingbar
and tail patches.
Woodland. Resident.

◄ Redpoll *Acanthis flammea* 13cm. Red head, black bib, no white on forked tail. Male has pink breast. Twittering call. Sings in spring, circling slowly above trees. Resident.

► Bullfinch *Pyrrhula pyrrhula* 15cm. Large, plump finch with conspicuous white rump, black wings and tail. Heavy bill, black cap. Male has bright red breast. Soft, piping whistle. Woodland. Resident.

♂ Summer

♂ Winter

▲ Chaffinch *Fringilla coelebs* 15cm. Double white wingbar, white outer tail feathers. Male slate-blue head, pink breast. Female greenish-brown. Common resident.

◄ Crossbill *Loxia curvirostra* 16cm. Heavy crossed bill. Short forked tail, wings and tail dark. Male is bright red, female greenish, plumage streaked. Coniferous woodland. Feeds on cones. Resident.

57

Buntings and Sparrows

▶ **Corn Bunting** *Emberiza calandra* 18cm. Like large sparrow, with heavy, stout bill. Pale brown with streaked plumage, no white on tail. Bill and legs yellowish. Resident.

♂ ♀

◀ **Yellowhammer** *Emberiza citrinella* 16cm. Chestnut rump, white outer tail feathers. Male has yellow head and underparts, female browner. Open country. Resident.

♂

♀

▶ **Cirl Bunting** *Emberiza cirlus* 16cm. Olive-brown rump. Male has black throat. Stripe through eye. Resident.

♀ ♂

◀ **Ortolan Bunting** *Emberiza hortulana* 16cm. Yellow throat, yellow ring round eye, grey head and chest. Female paler, streaked chest. Passage migrant.

▶ **Snow Bunting** *Plectrophenax nivalis* 16cm. White underparts, white patches on wing and tail. Male, summer: head white, back black. Winter: head brown, back brown, streaked black like female and young. On moors in summer. On coast in winter. Resident.

♀ ♂ Winter

♂ Summer

♂ Summer

♂ Winter

♀

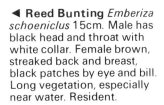

◀ **Reed Bunting** *Emberiza schoeniclus* 15cm. Male has black head and throat with white collar. Female brown, streaked back and breast, black patches by eye and bill. Long vegetation, especially near water. Resident.

♂

♀

▶ **Rock Bunting** *Emberiza cia* 16cm. Chestnut-red, dark wings and tail, grey head, striped crown. Female paler and duller. Outer tail feathers white. Not in Britain.

♀

♂

♂ Italian sparrow

◀ **House Sparrow** *Passer domesticus* 15cm. Male with grey crown, whitish underparts, black throat. Female has pale eye stripe. Chirps monotonously. Found chiefly in towns and villages. Resident.

◀ **Tree Sparrow** *Passer montanus* 14cm. Sexes similar, more brightly coloured than house sparrow, with chestnut crown, white cheeks with black spot. Occurs more in country than house sparrow. Open woodland, hedgerows. Resident.

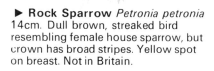

▶ **Rock Sparrow** *Petronia petronia* 14cm. Dull brown, streaked bird resembling female house sparrow, but crown has broad stripes. Yellow spot on breast. Not in Britain.

59

Amphibians and Reptiles

Amphibians and reptiles are animals which have backbones and are 'cold-blooded', which means they are unable to regulate their body temperature. Their activity depends on the temperature, so in cold weather, especially in winter, they become inactive.

Reptiles are adapted to living on land by their hard, scaly skins, which do not grow and are shed from time to time. The reptiles of northern Europe are divided into snakes and lizards. Snakes have no legs, but 'walk' on numerous ribs, the large scales on the belly stretching right across to help movement. Their jaws are hinged so that they can be opened widely to swallow large prey. Most lizards have four legs, and a tail that can be regrown if damaged. Most snakes and lizards lay eggs, but some, including the viper or adder and the slow-worm, produce active young. Amphibians include the frogs, toads and newts. They have soft skins, kept moist by glands and by living in damp places. Eggs are laid in water and the young (tadpoles) breathe with gills and have tails. Frogs and toads have no tails as adults; newts have long tails flattened sideways.

◀ **European Tree Frog** *Hyla meridionalis* 5cm. Small, bright green back, large suckers on finger tips. Not in Britain.

CLUES AND HINTS

When to look: Reptiles and amphibians are found more easily during the summer when they are active. In winter, they hide under stones or in crevices, often appearing dead.

Where to look: In spring, amphibians breed in large numbers in ponds. Remember to watch quietly.

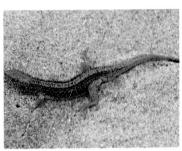

◀ **Green Lizard** *Lacerta viridis* Up to 13cm. Long-tailed lizard. Green back, light-yellow underparts. Lives in southern Europe.

Lizards and Snakes

▶ **Sand Lizard** *Lacerta agilis*
Body 9cm, tail 9cm. Male is green
on sides, especially in spring,
female brown or grey. Both
spotted. Young hatch from eggs
early summer. Coastal sand dunes,
heaths.

◀ **Common Lizard** *Lacerta
vivipara* Body 6.5cm, tail 7cm.
Brown or grey back, white,
orange, yellow or reddish below.
Young born alive, not hatching
from eggs. Grassy and heathy
places.

▶ **Slow-worm** *Anguis fragilis*
50cm. Snake-like, but really a
lizard without legs. Very smooth.
Young golden with dark back
stripe and belly. Eats slugs and
other small animals. Grassy places.

◀ **Grass Snake** *Natrix natrix*
120cm. Eye has round pupil. Grey,
green or brown, black spots or
markings down sides. Usually has
yellow collar. Young hatch from
eggs. Grassy places.

▶ **Adder** *Vipera berus* 65cm.
Head triangular, eye with
slit-like pupil. Grey or brown,
usually with zig-zag. Young
born alive, not from eggs.
Only poisonous snake in
Britain. Many habitats.

◀ **Smooth Snake** *Coronella
austriaca* 60cm. Small head, eyes
with round pupil. Often a dark line
from snout to eye. Young born
alive (not hatched from eggs) in
late summer. Eats mainly lizards.
Sandy heathland. Few areas in
southern Britain.

61

Frogs and Newts

▶ **Common Frog** *Rana temporaria* 10cm. Skin smooth, moist brown patch round ear drum. Hops on long legs. Colour variable with darker spots.

▼ **Edible Frog** *Rana esculenta* 12cm. Whitish vocal sacs bulge from throat when male croaks. More aquatic than common frog. Small colonies in southern England.

Tadpole

▼ **Natterjack Toad** *Bufo calamita* 8cm. Smaller than common toad, head narrower, eyes closer. Brown, grey or green with bright yellow stripe down back. Mainly in sandy and heathy areas.

◀ **Common Toad** *Bufo bufo* 15cm. Skin dry, warty, rough. Large cheek glands. Colour variable, brown, grey or green. Active at night. Damp places.

▶ **Midwife Toad** *Alytes obstetricans* 5cm. Small toad, short legs. Grey or brown. Male carries eggs in spring, dipping them in water to keep moist until ready to hatch. Hides in holes during day, active at night.

▼ ►Smooth Newt *Triturus vulgaris*
8–11cm. Smooth skin, with 3 grooves
on head. Throat and belly yellow or
orange, usually spotted. Pale brown
above. Male darker, in spring has large
spots and wavy crest from head to tail.
Found in water in spring.

▼ Warty Newt *Triturus cristatus*
11–15cm. Skin rough, dark above,
reddish-orange below with large
black blotches. In spring, male has
crest with sharp points.

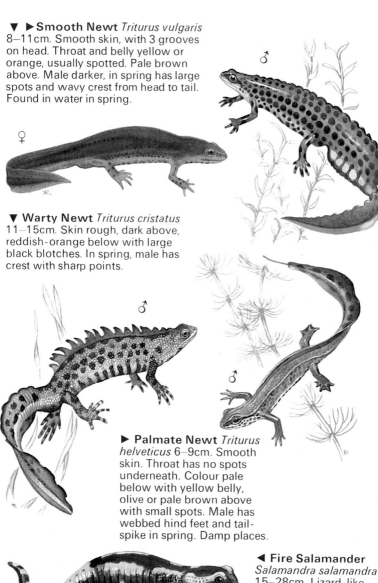

► Palmate Newt *Triturus
helveticus* 6–9cm. Smooth
skin. Throat has no spots
underneath. Colour pale
below with yellow belly,
olive or pale brown above
with small spots. Male has
webbed hind feet and tail-
spike in spring. Damp places.

◄ Fire Salamander
Salamandra salamandra
15–28cm. Lizard-like
with short tail.
Distinctive black or
yellow spots and
stripes. Young born
alive. Not in Britain.

63

Fishes

Fishes are animals with backbones that live in water. They have strong jaws, streamlined bodies generally covered in scales, and fins specialized for swimming. A powerful tail acts as a propeller, and the dorsal and anal fins keep the fish on a straight course. More primitive fishes, like the shark, have skeletons made of cartilages, but most are bony fishes, which have a skeleton made of many bones.

The pectoral and pelvic fins of bony fishes are in pairs and help to stabilize the fish as well as acting as brakes. In most species, a distinct line can be seen down the side of the body – this is known as the lateral line, and it contains sense organs that detect movement in the water. An air bladder inside the body helps to make the fish buoyant, so that it can keep its position in the water without having to go down to the bottom to rest. Bony fishes usually produce many eggs and the male normally sheds 'milt' on them to fertilize them.

The bony fishes are divided into two main groups, the soft-rayed fishes and the spiny-rayed fishes. Soft-rayed fishes have soft fins and include members of the salmon and carp families, the eel, loach, herring, pike, cod and smelt. Spiny-rayed fish, with sharp spines especially on the dorsal fins, include perch, bass, flat fish, gobies, blennies, bullheads, sand eels and scorpion fish.

External Features of a Fish

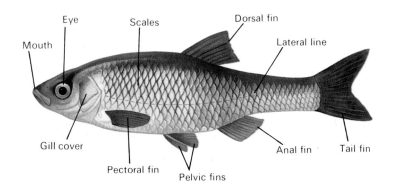

Eye

Scales

Dorsal fin

Lateral line

Mouth

Gill cover

Pectoral fin

Pelvic fins

Anal fin

Tail fin

All these fish breathe by passing water over their gills, taking it through the mouth and expelling it through the gill covers. The gills have a rich supply of blood vessels which extract oxygen from the water. Fish vary in the amount of oxygen they need, trout requiring well-oxygenated water to survive, while fish such as the carp need far less oxygen and can live in more stagnant water. Some species can even survive a great range of conditions. Migrating fish, like the salmon and sea trout, start life in fresh water, spending two or three years in the river in which they hatched before descending to the salt sea. They spend the next year or two there, adapting easily to saltwater conditions. When mature, they return again to the freshwater river to spawn. The eel, on the other hand, familiar as a young elver and adult eel in fresh water, returns to the sea to breed.

◀ **River Lamprey**
Lampetra fluviatilis
13–50cm. Belongs to a group of fish-like animals. A sucking mouth enables it to attach itself to the fish on which it feeds.

CLUES AND HINTS

Where to look: You can see freshwater fishes in rivers, canals, ponds, lakes and streams and small marine fishes in shallow water and rock pools on the coast, but they are very difficult to observe closely.

Colour changes: Many males alter their colour during the breeding season. Salmon and sea trout, for example, develop red and pinkish bellies and the grayling's dorsal fin turns red.

What to look for: Some fish are very good at camouflage. A common device is counter-shading, where the back is dark, the belly and sides light or silvery. Spots break up the outline of the sea trout and the mackerel has ripple markings, making both hard to see.

How to look: Be very quiet and still when watching fish. Don't let your shadow fall on the water as this can disturb them.

Freshwater Fishes

◄ **Salmon** *Salmo salar* Up to 150cm. Fish from sea, silvery, back darker, few small black spots. Breeding male has hooked jaw. Leaps out of water when travelling up river to lay eggs (spawn).

▶ **Brown Trout** *Salmo trutta* Up to 100cm. Colour brown with lighter belly, spotted red and black. Young trout easily confused with young salmon but pectoral fin orange. Common in fresh water.

◄ **Rainbow Trout** *Salmo gairdneri* Up to 70cm. Colour varies, but always with reddish iridescent band along side, heavily spotted all over including tail. Introduced from North America to lakes and ponds in Britain.

▶ **Grayling** *Thymallus thymallus* 50cm. Long striped dorsal fin, turns red on male in breeding season. Swims in shoals in swift streams. Feeds mainly on insect larvae on stream bed.

◄ **Pike** *Esox lucius* 40– 100cm. Long duck-like snout, sharp backward pointing teeth. Eats mainly other fishes. Lakes, ponds and rivers with weed growth.

► **Perch** *Perca fluviatilis* Up to 30cm. Dorsal fin spiny. Colour greenish-yellow with dark bands. Often living in shoals in rivers, lakes and ponds with weed growth.

◄ **Stone Loach** *Noemacheilus barbatulus* Up to 20cm. 4 'whiskers' (barbels) round mouth. Active at night in cool, clear lakes and streams. Feeds on other small animals.

► **Three Spined Stickleback** *Gasterosteus aculeatus* Up to 10cm. 3 spines on back with non-spiny fin behind. Spines on belly. Ponds and rivers and sometimes in the sea. The similar Ten spined stickleback *Pungitius pungitius* has 7 to 12, although generally 9, spines on back.

◄ **Eel** *Anguilla anguilla* Up to 100cm. Long, ribbon-like, with dorsal fin extending to tail and anal fin similar below. Yellow-brown in colour until ready to migrate to the sea to breed, when it becomes black with silver belly. It can travel overland.

► **Bullhead** *Cottus gobio* 8–10cm. A spiny fish with a broad, heavy head. Hides under stones in fresh running water.

67

Freshwater Fishes

▶ **Roach** *Rutilus rutilus* Up to
30cm. Back dark green, blue or
brown, sides and belly silvery-
white. One of the commonest
fishes in still and slow-moving
waters.

◀ **Carp** *Cyprinus
carpio* Up to 100cm. 4
'whiskers' by mouth.
Body thick, covered in
large scales. Still or
slow-moving water.
Active mainly by night.

▶ **Dace** *Leuciscus leuciscus* Up
to 20cm. Sometimes has golden
sheen on belly. Lower fins pink or
yellowish. Occurs in shoals in
fast-flowing water.

◀ **Tench** *Tinca tinca* Up to
25cm. 2 'whiskers' by mouth.
Eyes small, red. Skin slimy,
olive to black in colour.
Golden ornamental variety.
Weedy and muddy ponds and
slow-moving rivers.

▼ **Silver Bream** *Blicca bjoerkna*
Up to 30cm. Body flattened
sideways. Long anal fin. Small
head, tail deeply forked. Colour
silvery with greenish back.
Deep water.

▲ **Common Bream**
Abramis brama 30–50cm.
Deep body, flattened
sideways. Young bream
silvery. Quiet deep waters,
often in shoals.

► **Rudd** *Scardinius erythrophthalmus* 20–30cm. In warm, shallow waters with plenty of weeds. Feeds on plants and animals.

◄ **Chub** *Leuciscus cephalus* Up to 20cm. Mouth large. Male has white spots on head in spring. Common in running water, often in large shoals. Eats all kinds of water creatures and leaps out at flying insects.

► **Minnow** *Phoxinus phoxinus* Up to 10cm. Brown or green on back with yellow stripe down side. Silver below, but male has red belly in spring. Cool, clean water with sand or gravel bottom. In shoals.

◄ **Gudgeon** *Gobio gobio* Up to 15cm. 2 'whiskers' by mouth. Blotches on sides. Lives on bottom of sandy or gravelly fast-flowing rivers. Occasionally in lakes. Eats other animals.

► **Barbel** *Barbus barbus* Up to 50cm. 4 large 'whiskers' by mouth. Thick lips. Belly flattened beneath. Lives in shoals near bottom of fast-flowing rivers.

69

Coastal Fishes

▶ **Cod** *Gadus morhua* Up to
100cm. 3 dorsal, 2 anal fins.
'Whisker' on lower jaw. Greenish-
yellow or brown. Cold waters.

◀ **Bass** *Dicentrarchus
labrax* Up to 80cm. 2
dorsal fins, front one
spiny. Spines on gill
covers. Coastal waters.

▶ **Whiting** *Merlangius
merlangus* Up to 50cm. 3 dorsal,
2 anal fins. Dark spot at base of
pectoral fin. Dark grey or blue
back. Coastal waters, especially
over muddy bottoms.

◀ **Dab** *Limanda limanda* Up
to 40cm. Dorsal and anal fins
along length of body which is
flattened, right side
uppermost. Dark brown,
yellowish or grey below. Lies
flat on sand in coastal waters.

▶ **Flounder** *Platichthys flesus*
Up to 50cm. Fins as dab along
length of body, right side
uppermost. Rows of rough warts
on lateral line and base of fins.
Olive-brown or brown above.
Sandy coasts and estuaries.

◀ **Plaice** *Pleuronectes
platessa* Up to 60cm. Dorsal
and anal fins along length of
body. Flattened body has
right side uppermost. Brown
with red spots. Sandy coasts
and estuaries, often in deep
water.

► Common Goby
Pomatoschistus microps Up to 11cm. Short blunt head, large eyes close together. Very well camouflaged in sandy pools in which it lives.

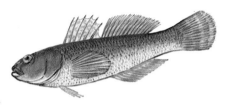

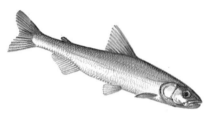

◄ Sand Smelt *Atherina presbyter* Up to 20cm. Small silvery fish with olive-green back and silvery-white stripe along sides. Scales outlined with black points. Lives in shoals on sandy bottoms in calm bays and estuaries.

► Montagu's Blenny
Coryphoblennius galerita Up to 10cm. Round head with two tentacles and flap of skin above eyes. Long dorsal fin dipping in middle. Mottled appearance gives camouflage in rocks pools.

◄ Scorpion Fish *Taurulus bubalis* Up to 15cm. Large head, flattened body. Large pectoral fins, 5 spines on gill covers. Brown blotches on paler background match the seaweed in which it lives. Common in shore pools.

► Greater Sand Eel
Hyperoplus lanceolatus Up to 30cm. Eel-like body, greenish above, pale below, with silvery line on sides. Dorsal fin continuous along back. Lower jaw long, used for burrowing in sand when disturbed. Often in shoals over sandy bottoms.

71

Insects and other Invertebrates

The largest group in the animal kingdom is the invertebrates – animals without backbones. This group includes the insects, with their tough outer skeleton, a segmented body and joined limbs. Most of them can fly. The body is divided into three distinct parts: the head, thorax and abdomen. The thorax has three pairs of legs attached to it, and usually two pairs of wings – except the true flies, which have only one pair, and others which have none at all. Some insects have both pairs of wings the same size, others have larger forewings than hindwings. The forewings of beetles are very tough and form a protective shield for the body.

The life history of insects varies considerably, but there are two main types. In one form, the young resemble small adults (nymphs), and shed their skins and grow until the adult winged stage is reached. The other form has completely different adult and young types. An example is the butterfly, which changes from a caterpillar (larva) to a pupa, then into the adult winged insect. Insects are classified in different orders according to their life histories and structure of their wings and mouth parts. They are so numerous that only a selection of species has been illustrated in the following pages.

External Features of an insect (side view)

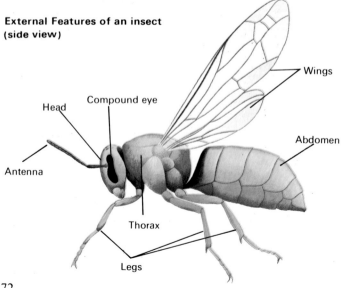

Wings

Head

Compound eye

Abdomen

Antenna

Thorax

Legs

▲ **Silver Y Moth** *Plusia gamma* 4cm. Brown-coloured moth, white Y on forewings. Summer visitor to Britain.

▲ **Praying Manis** *Mantis religiosa* Up to 7cm. Green or brown front legs adapted for catching prey. Not in Britain.

The kind of food an insect eats affects the shape of its mouth parts. Moths and butterflies, for example, have a long tongue (proboscis) used for sucking nectar, while locusts have cutting mouth parts for gnawing at leaves. Yet insects are constantly in danger of being eaten themselves by other animals. Some protect themselves by camouflage, like the patterned wings of certain moths which make them impossible to see against the bark of trees, some are brightly coloured to warn off predators and some sting, bite or release poison. Shape can be a camouflage too: there are insects which look like twigs, leaves, grass and even seeds.

CLUES AND HINTS

Where to look: Insects are everywhere, on earth and in water, on grass and flowers, on leaves and tree bark, even in houses. Look carefully at old trees, hedges and on ponds, where you will find more species than in gardens. **When to look:** There are more insects about in the summer months, but they can be found all year round.

How to look: Insects are small and often move very fast, so they are difficult to observe. Choose a small patch of territory and learn to look closely for a long time. The insect may be hiding under a leaf or flat against a twig, protecting itself from predators. Jot down all the details you can and do an accurate drawing.

Butterflies

All measurements are
across a single forewing

▶ **Swallowtail** *Papilio
machaon* 32–38mm. Large
butterfly with black and
yellow pattern. Flight strong
and quick. Caterpillar green
with black rings, yellow spots,
feeding on milk parsley.

▶ **Small White** *Pieris rapae*
20–26mm. Similar to large
white, smaller size. Male 1 to
2 black spots, female 3.
Hindwing underside is yellow.
Caterpillar green with yellow
stripe. Common everywhere
in summer.

◀ **Large White** *Pieris brassicae*
29–34mm. Similar to small white.
Female 2 black spots on forewing.
Male without such spots.

▶ **Orange Tip** *Anthocharis
cardamines* 21–25mm. Male
distinctive orange patch on tip of
forewing; hindwing patchy grey.
Female similar with no orange
patch; hindwing strongly mottled.
Caterpillar green. Common woods
and hedgerows.

◀ **Clouded Yellow**
Colias crocea 23–
27mm. Female has
yellow spots on
black border.
Summer visitor.

▶ **Brimstone**
Gonepteryx rhamni
26–30mm. Male
brilliant yellow with red
spots. Female yellowish-
green. Green caterpillar.

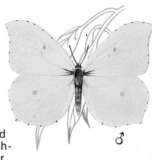

▶ **Peacock** *Inachis io* 27–35mm. Attractive butterfly with 'peacock' eyes on wings. Female slightly larger. Underside dark brown. Flight strong, direct. Caterpillar black, feeds on nettles. Common everywhere.

◀ **Purple Emperor** *Apatura iris* 31–37mm. Large dark butterfly, usually flies in tree tops. Female larger and without purple. Caterpillar green with yellow stripes. Deciduous woodland.

▶ **White Admiral** *Limenitis camilla* 26–30mm. Undersides yellowish-brown. Caterpillar yellowish-green. Feeds on honeysuckle. Deciduous woodlands.

◀ **Red Admiral** *Vanessa atalanta* 28–31mm. Underside forewing pattern paler; hindwing patches dark and light brown. Black caterpillar, yellow stripe, feeds on nettles.

▶ **Painted Lady** *Vanessa cardui* 27–29mm. A migrant, arriving in Europe from N. Africa in spring and spreading all over Europe in summer.

75

Butterflies

▶ **Small Tortoiseshell** *Aglais urticae* 22–25mm. Abundant in gardens. It hibernates and flies early in spring. Spiky black caterpillar feeds on nettles.

◀ **Camberwell Beauty** *Nymphalis antiopa* 30–35mm. Broad yellow, or whitish edges to wings. Rare visitor to Britain.

▶ **Comma** *Polygonia c-album* 22–24mm. Easily recognized by jagged edge to wings. Underside dark, with white C on hindwing. Woodland edges, hedgerows and gardens.

◀ **Silver-washed Fritillary** *Argynnis paphia* 33–38mm. Underside hindwing greenish with silver stripes. Woodland clearings.

▶ **Heath Fritillary** *Mellicta athalia* 18–20mm. Orange-brown and yellow markings give a chequered appearance. Underside paler, hindwings whitish. Flowery meadows and open woodland.

◀ **Pearl-bordered Fritillary** *Clossiana euphrosyne* 19–23mm. Similar in size to heath fritillary, spotted not chequered. Underside of hindwing has silver spots. Open grassland, heaths and woodland glades.

▲ Ringlet *Aphantopus hyperantus* 20–24mm. Male dark brown. Female light brown. Underside of both sexes usually has 7 black spots, circled in white. Hedgerows and woodland areas.

▲ Marbled White *Melanargia galathea* 23–26mm. Underside paler. Meadows and rough grassland, early summer.

♀

◄ Meadow Brown *Maniola jurtina* 22–25mm. Male has smaller orange patches, often none at all. Underside hindwing has broad pale band. Grasslands.

► Small Heath *Coenonympha pamphilus* 14–17mm. Underside hindwing grey or blue-brown with white mark. Common on open grassland.

► Speckled Wood *Pararge aegeria* 19–22mm. Dark brown with large cream spots. Underside similar. Caterpillar feeds on grasses. Open woodland.

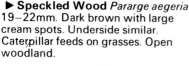

◄ Wall Butterfly *Lasiommata megera* 19–25mm. Rich orange-brown. Underside pale and spotted. Caterpillar feeds on grasses. Roadsides and hedgerows.

Butterflies

♀

◄ Purple Hairstreak
Quercusia quercus 12–
14mm. Male much
more purple. Underside
light grey with white
lines. Oak woodland.

► Green Hairstreak
Callophrys rubi 13–
15mm. Underside
bright green with white
lines or spots. Heaths
with gorse and broom.

► Common Blue
Polyommatus icarus
14–18mm. Female
brown, tinged with
blue, orange border to
wings. Underside light
grey with black and
white spots. Grasslands.

♂

◄ Brown Argus
Aricia agestis 12–
14mm. Dark brown
with orange border.
Underside grey-brown,
similar to common blue.
Grassy slopes.

▲ Small Blue *Cupido
minimus* 10–12mm.
Male brown, bluish
tinge to wings. Female
brown. Underside
greyish. Grassy slopes.

► Small Copper *Lycaena phlaeas*
12–15mm. Forewings orange-red
with dark brown border, small spots.
Underside of wings paler than top.
Common grassy slopes and heaths.
Caterpillar feeds on sorrel.

◄ Small Skipper
Thymelicus sylvestris 13–
15mm. Thick body. Black
mark on forewing of male.
Underside darker. Rapid
darting flight. Grassland.

► Grizzled Skipper *Pyrgus
malvae* 11–13mm. Underside
pale and blotched. Rapid,
darting flight. Caterpillar feeds
on strawberries, cinquefoil.
Grassland.

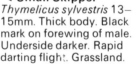

Moths

Measurements across forewing.
Male moths have feathery antennae.

▼ Death's Head Hawkmoth
Acherontia atropos 45–60mm.
Large, broad body, striped
abdomen. Occasional migrant
from abroad.

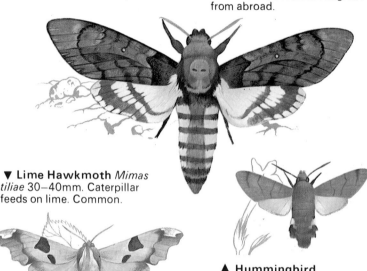

▼ Lime Hawkmoth *Mimas
tiliae* 30–40mm. Caterpillar
feeds on lime. Common.

**▲ Hummingbird
Hawkmoth** *Macroglossum
stellatarum* 20–30mm. Flies
during the day, hovering like a
hummingbird to suck nectar.

▶ Buff-tip Moth *Phalera
bucephala* 21–24mm. At rest,
wings fold like tent. Tufts at base
of wing form hump. Caterpillar
feeds on trees.

Caterpillar

Caterpillar

◀ Puss Moth *Cerura vinula* 28–
36mm. Body fluffy. Caterpillar can
puff up front end of body to look
frightening. Feeds on willow,
poplar.

79

Moths

▶ **Pale Tussock** *Calliteara pudibunda* 21–29mm. Female larger and paler. Caterpillar hairy, feeds on birch, hazel.

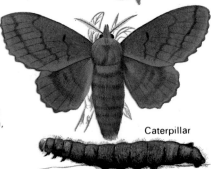

▲ **Drinker** *Philudoria potatoria* 30–35mm. Male reddish-brown, female yellower. Caterpillar has tufts of hairs. Damp grassland.

Caterpillar

◀ **Lackey** *Malacosoma neustria* 13–20mm. Small hairy moth. Caterpillars live in large numbers in a tent of silk.

▲ **Lappet** *Gastropacha quercifolia* 27–43mm. Body large, hairy. Looks like a dead leaf at rest.

▶ **Emperor** *Saturnia pavonia* 28–40mm. Female grey. Male smaller and browner. Flies by day. Caterpillar green with black rings. Feeds on brambles and other shrubs.

▼ **Garden Tiger** *Arctia caja* 37mm. Stout hairy body. Caterpillar hairy, feeds on many plants including nettles. Common.

Caterpillar

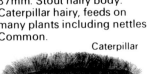

▶ **Cinnabar** *Tyria jacobaeae* 18–21mm. Brightly coloured. Caterpillar orange and black, common on ragwort.

▶ **Buff Ermine** *Spilosoma lutea* 20–25mm. Stout hairy body. Caterpillar brown, hairy. Common.

80

▶ Large Yellow Underwing
Noctua pronuba 20–29mm.
Hides underwings when at rest.
Caterpillar feeds on grasses, docks,
cabbage. Common.

◀ Red Underwing
Catocala nupta 35–
40mm. Forewings cover
hindwings at rest,
hiding the moth.
Caterpillar feeds on
poplars.

◀ Large Emerald
Geometra papilionaria
18–20mm. A number
of similar, but smaller,
species occur, differing
in markings and shape.
Caterpillar is a 'looper'

◀ Magpie *Abraxas
grossulariata* 17–
21mm. Markings on
wings vary but black
and white spots with
orange patches are
distinctive. Caterpillar
is a 'looper', feeds on
fruit bushes.

▲ Garden Carpet
Xanthorhoe fluctuata
12–15mm. Slender
body. Caterpillar is a
'looper'.

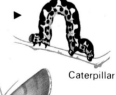

▶

Caterpillar

♀

▲ Peppered Moth *Biston
betularia* 19–22mm. A black form
became widespread in industrial
areas when smoke pollution was a
problem. Caterpillar is a 'looper' on
oak, elm, poplar and other trees.

▲ Bordered White *Bupalus
piniaria* 19–22mm. Male pale
yellow or white. Female wings
more orange. Caterpillar feeds on
pine needles.

81

Moths

▶ **Six-spot Burnet** *Zygaena filipendulae* 14–18mm. Antennae with clubbed ends. Flies by day. Caterpillar feeds on bird's-foot trefoil. Grassland.

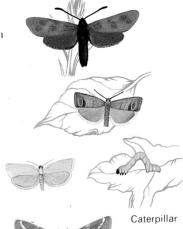

▶ **Codlin Moth** *Cydia pomonella* 7–9mm. Small moth with square forewings. Caterpillar often a pest, feeding on apples and pears.

▶ **Green Tortrix** *Tortrix viridana* 9–11 mm. Small moth with square, green forewings. Caterpillars feed on oaks.

Caterpillar

▶ **Common Swift Moth** *Hepialus lupulina* 12–15mm. Short antennae. Fast-flying. White marks often absent, especially on female. Caterpillar often a pest, eating roots of plants.

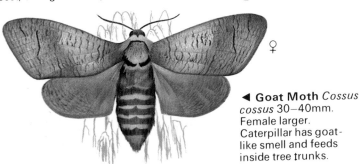

♀

◀ **Goat Moth** *Cossus cossus* 30–40mm. Female larger. Caterpillar has goat-like smell and feeds inside tree trunks.

◀ **Hornet Clearwing** *Sesia apiformis* 15–20mm. Resembles wasp but is not narrow in middle. Caterpillar feeds in poplar trunks.

▶ **Plume Moth** *Pterophorus pentadactylus* 12–14mm. Narrow wings are divided into feather-like, white plumes. Weak, jerky flight. Caterpillar feeds on bindweed.

Beetles

Measurements = length

▲ **Violet Ground Beetle** *Carabus violaceus* 18–34mm. Forewings black with violet sheen. Long legs and large jaws.

▶ **Green Tiger Beetle** *Cicindela campestris* 12–15mm. Runs after prey in sunshine and catches it with large jaws. Flies well.

♂

◀ **Whirligig Beetle** *Gyrinus natator* 5–7mm. Small, freshwater beetle. Whirls round on water surface.

◀ **Great Diving Beetle** *Dysticus marginalis* 35mm. Carnivorous beetle, living in ponds and rivers. Female has striped wings. Male has suckers on front legs.

▲ **Devil's Coach Horse** *Staphylinus olens* 20–25mm. Forewings very short. When disturbed, curls abdomen over back like a scorpion.

▶ **Burying Beetle** *Nicrophorus humator* 18–28mm. Antennae with orange clubbed ends. Buries carrion for larvae to eat.

♀

◀ **Cockchafer** *Melolontha melolontha* 20–30mm. Blundering flight, attracted to light at dusk. Adults eat foliage.

▶ **Fur Beetle** *Attagenus pellio* 45–50mm. Often found in houses. Larvae eat and damage fur and carpets.

◀ **Click Beetle** *Ctenicera cuprea* 11–16mm. If on its back, makes a loud click as it jumps to right itself. Lives in grassland.

♂

▲ **Stag Beetle** *Lucanus cervus* Male 60–70mm, female 30–40mm. Mouthparts enlarged in male into horn-like structures. Flies in evening.

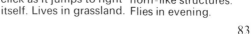

83

Beetles

► Wasp Beetle
Clytus arietis 18–25mm. Wasp-like, but harmless. Scuttles over leaves and tree trunks.

▲ Colorado Beetle
Leptinotarsa decemlineata 6–11mm. A potato pest from America. Larvae are pink and fleshy. Adults and larvae eat potato leaves.

► Nut Weevil
Curculio nucum 6–7mm. Long snout, especially in female. Female bores a hole with snout to lay eggs. Larvae feed inside hazel nuts.

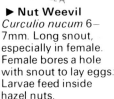

◄ Death Watch Beetle *Xestobium rufovillosum* 5–8mm. Head small, rounded, almost covered by shield on thorax. Male makes clicking sound (April, May) to attract female. Larvae destructive, boring into timbers of old buildings.

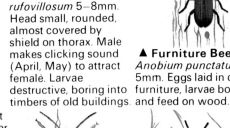

▲ Mealworm Beetle
Tenebrio molitor 10–17mm. Forewings have long parallel grooves. Larvae live in flour, a pest in stores and mills.

◄ Cardinal Beetle
Pyrochroa coccinea 20–25mm. A flat beetle with feathery antennae. Often seen on flowers. Larvae are carnivorous.

▲ Furniture Beetle
Anobium punctatum 3–5mm. Eggs laid in cracks or furniture, larvae bore holes and feed on wood.

▲ Tortoise Beetle
Cassida viridis 7–10mm. At rest, the broad front wings and head shield are pulled down to completely conceal the body. Feeds on various leaves.

▼ Oil Beetle *Meloe proscarabaeus* Male 10mm female 36mm. Short forewings. Exudes oil when disturbed.

◄ Seven-spot Ladybird *Coccinella 7-punctata* 7–8mm. Hard, red forewings with 7 black spots. Larvae like bluish woodlice. Both adults and larvae feed on aphids.

Bugs

► **Pondskater** *Gerris lacustris* 10–13mm. Long, thin legs for gliding on surface film of fresh water. 1st pair used for catching prey, 2nd pair for skating, 3rd pair for steering. Ponds and lakes.

◄ **Water Boatman** *Corixa punctata* 13–16mm. Long, flattened hind legs for swimming under water.

▼ **Hawthorn Shield Bug** *Acanthosoma haemorrhoidale* 10–13mm. Triangular-shaped shield covers bases of forewings. Feeds on hawthorn fruit and leaves.

► **Assassin Bug** *Reduvius personatus* 18–23mm. Curved piercing mouthparts for sucking juice from prey. Feeds on other insects. Larva covers itself with scraps of rubbish to hide.

► **Leaf Hopper** *Jassus lanio* 6–8mm. Sucks sap of oak leaves. Leaps well. One of many similar species.

▲ **Southern Cicada** *Cicadetta montana* 16–27mm. Normally rests with wings folded, in trees and shrubs. Very difficult to see, but male makes shrill whistle. Nymphs feed on tree roots.

◄ **Frog Hopper** *Philaenus spumarius* 5–6mm. Jumps well. Nymphs develop in 'cuckoo spit'.

▼ **Rose Aphid (Greenfly)** *Macrosiphum rosae* 2–3mm. Similar to blackfly, but green. Infests various plants and spreads diseases.

▲ **Greenhouse Whitefly** *Trialeurodes vaporariorum* 1–4mm. Small, white sucking bugs with white waxy wings. Occur on undersides of leaves in greenhouses.

▲ **Blackfly** *Aphis fabae* 2–3mm. Round black bugs with long legs and antennae. Winged or wingless. Females can reproduce without mating. Spreads diseases to various crops.

85

Ants and Bees

▲ **Dark Ant** *Formica fusca* 10–15mm. Head narrow, round at back. Common in gardens especially under paved paths.

▲ **Black Ant** *Lasius niger* 3–5mm. Small ant. Common in gardens.

▲ **Wood Ant** *Formica rufa* 5–11mm. Builds large mounds, especially in pine woods.

► **Honey Bee** *Apis mellifera* 12–20mm. Thousands of female worker bees live in a colony with one queen. Male bees have no sting.

▼ **White-tailed Bumblebee** *Bombus lucorum* 20–24mm. Black and yellow stripes with white end. Builds nest underground, often in an old mouse hole.

◄ **Cuckoo Bee** *Nomada lineola* 10–12mm. Small bee, looking like wasp. Lays eggs in nests of mining bees.

▼ **Mining Bee** *Andrena fulva* 10–12mm. Male dark, female rich brown. Abdomen flattened. Broad hind legs sweep earth. Digs nest burrow with mouth parts.

► **Leafcutter Bee** *Megachile centuncularis* 9–12mm. Resembles honey bee but darker striped abdomen. Cuts pieces from leaves, especially roses, to build nests.

Wasps

▶ **Common Wasp** *Vespula vulgaris*
11–20mm. One of several very similar
species. Builds nest from wood pulp
made into 'paper' by chewing. All die
in autumn except the new queens
which hibernate and start new nests
in spring.

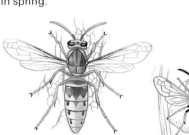

◀ **Hornet** *Vespa crabro* 19–
35mm. Large wasp. Brown not
black markings and deep yellow
colour. Papery nests made in
hollow trees.

◀ **Potter Wasp**
Eumenes coarctatus
15mm. Waist long and
narrow. Builds vase-
shaped nest from clay,
and puts caterpillars in
for its young to eat.

▼ **Digger Wasp** *Ammophila sabulosa* 16–
28mm. Very long, slender waist. Nests in
burrows in sandy soil.

▶ **Horntail** *Urocerus gigas*
10–40mm. No waist. Female
larger than male, with black
and yellow bands and large
egg-laying tube at hind end.
Larvae feed on wood.

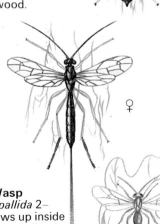

♂

♀

▶ **Ichneumon Fly** *Rhyssa
persuasoria* 30mm. Parasite with very
long slender egg-laying tube. Attacks
horntail larvae in wood.

▼ **Hawthorn Sawfly** *Trichiosoma
tibiale* 20mm. No waist. Female has
egg-laying tube, making slits in
plants in which to lay eggs.

▶ **Gall Wasp**
Biorthiza pallida 2–
3mm. Grows up inside
oak apple – a gall
growing on oak trees.

87

True Flies

► Bluebottle
Calliphora vomitoria
12mm. Large, buzzing
fly with shiny metallic
blue abdomen.

◄ Stable Fly
Stomoxys calcitrans
5–7mm. Spiky mouth
pierces skin of animals,
sucks blood.

► Hover Fly *Syrphus
ribesi* 10–12mm.
Usually seen on flowers
or hovering with rapidly
beating wings, often
going backwards.
Larvae feed on aphids.

◄ Bee Fly *Bombylius
major* 8–12mm. A furry,
bee-like fly. Sucks
nectar with long
tongue. Hovers.

▲ House Fly *Musca
domestica* 7–9mm.
Small dark fly;
mouthparts mop up
liquids. Larvae feed on
decaying animal matter.

► Midge *Chironomus
annularis* 11–15mm.
Non-biting midge.
Hump behind head.
Male has feathery
antennae.

▼ Mosquito *Culex
pipiens* 3–5mm. Male
has feathery antennae.
Female has pointed
mouthparts for sucking
blood.

♂

▲ Robber Fly *Asilus
crabroniformis* 16–30mm
Big eyes and strong, hairy
legs help it to catch other
insects in flight.

♂

► Crane Fly *Tipula
maxima* 15–23mm.
Male abdomen not
pointed. Some Crane
Fly larvae are pests
eating roots of grass.

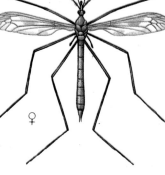

♀

Other Flies

▼ **Caddis Fly** *Phryganea grandis*
15–21mm. Long, spiky legs. Wings
hairy, held like a roof at rest, with
antennae pointing forwards. Near
water.

▲ **Scorpion Fly** *Panorpa
communis* 20mm. Beak-like
head. End of male's body
turned up like scorpion.
Shady places.

▼ **Mayfly** *Isonychia ignota*
15–20mm. 2 long 'tails',
hindwings small. Shortlived.
Near water. Not in Britain.

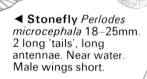

◀ **Stonefly** *Perlodes
microcephala* 18–25mm.
2 long 'tails', long
antennae. Near water.
Male wings short.

▲ **Lacewing** *Chrysopa
septempunctata* 30–40mm. Soft
green body, wings folded roof-like
at rest. Adults and larvae feed on
aphids.

▼ **Snake Fly**
Raphidia notata 25–
29mm. Long neck
readily identifies this
insect. Female has long
egg-laying tube.

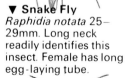

◀ **Alder Fly** *Sialis
lutaria* 25mm. Wings
held roof-like at rest.
Found near slow-
moving streams. Larvae
live in water.

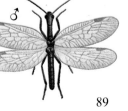

Dragonflies

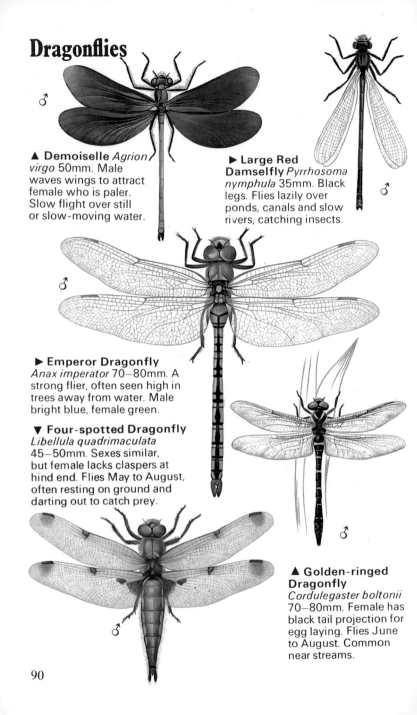

▲ **Demoiselle** *Agrion virgo* 50mm. Male waves wings to attract female who is paler. Slow flight over still or slow-moving water.

▶ **Large Red Damselfly** *Pyrrhosoma nymphula* 35mm. Black legs. Flies lazily over ponds, canals and slow rivers, catching insects.

▶ **Emperor Dragonfly** *Anax imperator* 70–80mm. A strong flier, often seen high in trees away from water. Male bright blue, female green.

▼ **Four-spotted Dragonfly** *Libellula quadrimaculata* 45–50mm. Sexes similar, but female lacks claspers at hind end. Flies May to August, often resting on ground and darting out to catch prey.

▲ **Golden-ringed Dragonfly** *Cordulegaster boltonii* 70–80mm. Female has black tail projection for egg laying. Flies June to August. Common near streams.

Other Insects

◄ Meadow Grasshopper
Chorthippus parallelus 11–24mm.
Forewings leathery, hindwings
minute. Colour variable. Male has
longer front wings and 'sings' by
rubbing legs against wings.

◄ House Cricket
Acheta domesticus
16–20mm. Wings of
male rubbed to produce
chirping 'song'. Female
has needle-like egg-
layer. Active at night.

► Field Cricket
Gryllus campestris 20–
25mm. Male produces
chirping 'song'. Female
has long tube for egg
laying. Lives in burrow.

► Oak Bush Cricket
Meconema thalassinum
15mm. Female has
broad, blade-like tube
for laying eggs. Flies
at night and often
attracted to lights.
Eats small insects.

**► Common
Cockroach** *Blatta
orientalis* 18–30mm.
Flat, dark brown or
black. Male has longer
wings. Active indoors
at night.

▲ Earwig *Forficula
auricularia* 14–23mm.
Forewings very short.
Pincers at end of
abdomen, curved in
male, straighter in
female.

▼ Cat Flea
Ctenocephalides felis
5mm. Hard body,
flattened from side to
side. No wings. Sucks
blood. Jumps well with
long hind legs.

▲ Silver Fish *Lepisma
saccharina* 7–10mm.
No wings, 3 'tails',
tapering silvery bodies
covered with dust-like
scales.

▲ Springtail *Podura
aquatica* 5mm. No
wings. Jumps forward.
On surface of ponds
and lakes.

► Bark louse 2mm. One of
many very similar small insects
that live on tree trunks. They
chew pollen grains and algae.

▼ Onion Thrips
Thrips tabaci 1–2mm.
Very small with 2 pairs
of feather-like wings.
Destructive to crops.

Other Invertebrates

◄ Garden Spider
Araneus diadematus.
Male 4–8mm, female
10–15mm. Weaves
circular, sticky webs on
bushes and fences.

► House Spider
Tegenaria domestica
10–15mm. A fast-
running spider, often
found indoors. Spins
cobwebs in corners.

▼ Water Spider
Argyroneta aquatica
10–15mm. Lives under
water in silken tent filled
with air. Reddish-
brown, often looks
silvery due to air trapped
on hairy body.

▲ Harvestman
Phalangium opilio
7–10mm. Not a true
spider. It has only 1
body section, spiders
have 2.

▲ Wolf Spider *Pisaura
mirabilis* 15–20mm.
Covers its eggs with a
tent-like web. Runs after
prey to catch it.

► Harvest Mite
Trombicula autumnalis
Less than 1mm. 8 legs,
round body, small head.

► Millipede
Ommatoiulus sabulosus
40–50mm. Body round
rather than flat. 2 pairs
of legs to each segment.
Feeds on plants.

▲ Centipede
Lithobius forficatus
25–40mm. Flat body,
with 1 pair of legs to
each segment. Feeds on
other animals.

◄ Earthworm
Lumbricus terrestris
90–200mm. No head
or legs, but front end is
more pointed.·

► Woodlouse *Oniscus asellus* 12–15mm. Land-living crustacean, with grey body and 7 pairs of legs. Always in damp places.

► Garden Slug *Arion subfuscus* 25–30mm. Long slimy body leaving trail behind. Back is rounded, brown in colour. Long tentacles show when moving.

◄ Medicinal Leech *Hirudo medicinalis* 35–70mm. Worm-like with powerful sucker at hind end. Mouth adapted for sucking blood. Fresh water.

◄ Freshwater Shrimp *Gammarus pulex* 15–20mm. Flattened from side to side. Lives at bottom of streams and ponds.

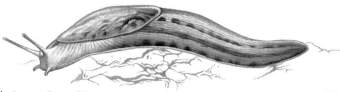

▲ Great Grey Slug *Limax maximus* 12–15cm. One of the larger slugs. Back keeled, not rounded. Feeds on rotting plants and fungi.

► Great Ram's Horn Snail *Planorbarius corneus* Shell 12–30mm across. Round, brown with 4 to 6 whorls. A pair of tentacles appear when snail moves. Lives in fresh water.

▲ Garden Snail *Helix aspersa* 25–35mm. Shell round with 4 to 5 right-handed whorls. Secretes slimy trail. Eyes at tops of longer tentacles.

◄ Great Pond Snail *Lymnaea stagnalis* 50–60mm. Shell tapers to fine point. One pair of tentacles show when moving. Eyes at base of tentacles. Fresh water.

Shells and other Seashore Creatures

Shells are the outer skeletons of soft-bodied animals belonging to a large group of animals called molluscs. The young are often completely different and swim freely before settling down to become adults – either on sandy shores or rocks. Most molluscs can be assigned to two main groups, the univalves (one shell or valve) and the bivalves (two shells or valves). Univalves develop one shell which may be coiled or dome-shaped. They include the snails and limpets. The soft-bodied mollusc fills the shell, and the part emerging from the base of the shell, known as the foot, is used for moving and feeding. Bivalves have two shells, joined together by a hinge, which interlocks and is toothed so that the two halves fit tightly together. Strong muscles close the shell when necessary. Bivalves all live in water and strain small particles of food from currents of water drawn into the shell.

Bivalve   Single shell (univalve)

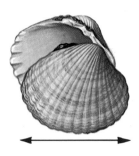
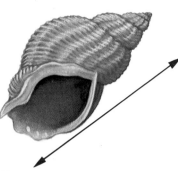

▲ Bivalves are usually measured by width and univalves by length.

Another smaller group of shells, of which the chiton is the most familiar, have a similar internal structure, but the shells are formed into a number of plates, enabling the animal to roll up in case of danger. The last group of molluscs either have very small shells or have lost them altogether. It includes squids and octopuses. Their shells are surrounded by their body. They use long arms with suckers to feed, and have a water-expelling siphon allowing them to swim rapidly when required.

94

As well as the molluscs, many other creatures can be found on the seashore. One of the largest groups is the crustaceans, which belongs to the same major division of animals as insects. They have a segmented body with a hard outer covering, antennae and legs. This group includes the familiar crab, lobster and shrimp, as well as the barnacle. Sea anemones and jellyfish belong to another group and are quite primitive animals with only a few layers of cells, some of which sting. Jellyfish swim, while anemones are fixed and wait for the sea currents to bring them food. The aquatic worms such as the ragworm and lugworm have long segmented bodies, with large heads and numerous bristles. Starfish and sea urchins, on the other hand, are wheel-shaped or globular and walk on special structures called tube feet, which project from their arms. Many of these animals are specialized in the way that they live and only occur on certain parts of the shore.

◀ **Crawfish** *Palinurus vulgaris* 50cm. Like the lobster in shape, but has no large claws on the first pair of legs. Reddish-brown with speckled legs and antennae. Lives in the warm waters of the Mediterranean and Atlantic coasts of Europe to the Channel.

CLUES AND HINTS

Where to look: Sandy shores are good places to look for bivalves, especially at low tide. On rocky shores, many different kinds of shells cling to rocks. Look in crevices and cracks and in pools. Search carefully on muddy shores and estuaries when the tide is out.

How to look: When studying live molluscs, treat them gently and always replace them where you found them. When collecting empty shells on the shore, keep a record of when and where you found them. Clean them and store carefully in cotton wool in labelled boxes.

Single Shells

▲ **Whelk** *Buccinum undatum* Up to 12cm long. 6 to 8 whorls separated by deep grooves. Common on muddy, rocky shores.

▶ **Necklace Shell** *Natica alderi* 1.5–3cm long. Rounded, smooth shell with short spiral coil. Common on sand below tide line.

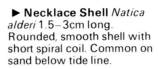

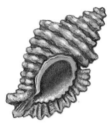

◀ **Sting Winkle** *Ocenebra erinacea* 6cm long. Pointed spiral shell. 4 to 7 whorls with rough, spiny projections. Common on firm bottoms, jetties, piers.

◀ **Pelican's Foot** *Aporrhais pes-pelecani* 5cm long. Thick shell with 10 to 12 whorls and with long pointed projections at base. Colour variable. Lives below tide line.

▶ **Chinaman's Hat** *Calyptraea chinensis* 7mm high. Low shell, flattened whorls. Attached to rocks, piers, jetties.

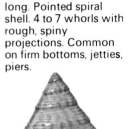

▲ **Painted Topshell** *Calliostoma zizyphinum* 4cm high. Pointed with close whorls. Reddish-yellow with red spots. Just below tide line.

◀ **Keyhole Limpet** *Fissurella costaria* 6cm wide. Flattened, low conical shell with prominent ribs radiating from the keyhole-shaped centre. Yellow-grey. Stony bottoms and rocks.

▲ **Common Limpet** *Patella vulgata* Up to 6cm wide. Greenish-white or brown with broad dark rays. Clings to rocks between tide lines on rocky coasts. Feeds and moves at night.

▶ **Slipper Limpet** *Crepidula fornicata* Up to 5cm wide. White plate inside extending across half the opening. Pest on oyster beds.

◄ European Cowrie *Trivia monacha* 4cm long. Small, finely-ribbed shell. White or pink. Rocky shores.

► Needle Shell
Bittium reticulatum 1.2cm long. Whorls have raised bumps forming spiral lines. Common in seaweed. Rocky and muddy shores.

◄ Wentletrap *Clathrus clathrus* 3cm long. 12 to 15 whorls with deep grooves between them crossed by thick ridges. Sandy, muddy shores.

► Tower Shell
Turritella communis 5cm long. Spiral lines follow the twist of the shell. Common muddy and sandy shores below low tide line.

▲ Common Periwinkle *Littorina littorea* 2–3cm long. Usually slate-coloured with darker spiral bands following the twist of the shell. Common on seaweed between tide lines.

◄ Flat Periwinkle *Littorina littoralis* 1.5cm. Shell rounded with flattened top. Few whorls. Colour variable. Occurs on shores where the seaweed bladderwrack grows.

► Ormer *Haliotis tuberculata* 6–8cm long. Flat, ear-shaped shell with line of holes near outer edge. Upper whorls tightly coiled. Brown, mother-of-pearl lining. Rocky shores.

▲ Chiton
Lepidochitona cinereus 2–4cm long. 8 overlapping plates enable animal to curl up. Colour variable. Common on or under stones near high tide line.

Bivalves

▶ **Oyster** *Ostrea edulis* Up to 15cm wide. Shell thick, brown, chalky. Shape irregular with heavy ridges. Cements itself to stony bottoms in shallow water, especially estuaries.

▶ **Saddle Oyster** *Anomia ephippium* Up to 6cm wide. Smaller than oyster. Orange-brown with white marks. Stony shore near low tide line.

▲ **Queen Scallop** *Chlamys opercularis* Up to 9cm wide. Shape almost circular, with flat hinge. 18–22 prominent ribs. Sandy shores, below low tide line.

◀ **Nut Shell** *Nucula nucleus* Up to 1.2cm wide. Small, thin, flat shell. Common offshore, burrowing in sand, mud or silt.

▶ **Cockle** *Cardium edule* 5cm wide. Harvested for food. Common sandy and muddy shores, estuaries.

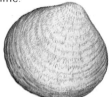

▲ **Dog Cockle** *Glycymeris glycymeris* 6–10cm wide. Almost circular, thick shell with grooved inner margins and humped hinge. Sandy shores.

◀ **Rayed Artemis** *Dosinia exoleta* Up to 5cm wide. Thick valves, pointed hinge. Common sandy and muddy shores, below low tide line.

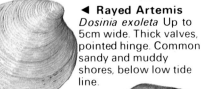

▲ **Mussel** *Mytilus edulis* 8cm wide. Blue-grey. White inside with blue edge, shiny. Common, anchored to rocks, jetties, piers.

▲ **Common Otter** *Lutraria lutraria* 13cm wide. Oblong valves, gaping open slightly at each end. Burrows in sand and mud. Common.

◄ Rayed Trough Shell *Mactra corallina* 6cm wide. Smooth, thin, triangular or oval. Hinge blunt. Common on sandy shores.

► Piddock *Pholas dactylus* 15cm wide. Valves long, finger-like at one end. Sharp teeth on edge. Bores holes in wood, soft rocks. Common.

▲ Sand Gaper *Mya arenaria* 12cm wide. Left valve smaller, valves do not close completely. Burrows in mud and sand. Common.

◄ Baltic Tellin *Tellina balthica* 2cm wide. Thin, rounded shell. Pointed hinge. Common on muddy shores.

► Blunt Tellin *Tellina crassa* 5cm wide. Shell thick, rounded. Sandy shores below low tide mark.

◄ Banded Wedge *Donax vittatus* 3cm wide. Oblong shape, shiny surface. Yellow to brown outside, purple, white or yellow inside. Sandy shores near low tide mark.

▲ Thin Tellin *Tellina tenuis* 2.5cm wide. Thin, oval valves, remaining together after the animal dies. Sandy shores near low tide mark.

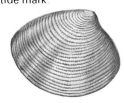

◄ Large Razor Shell *Ensis siliqua* 20cm long. Long, narrow, almost straight shell with hinge nearer to one end. Open at both ends. Burrows, living in holes on sandy shores. Common.

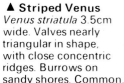

▲ Small Razor Shell *Ensis ensis* Up to 16cm long. Similar to large razor shell but smaller and more strongly curved. Burrows and lives in holes in sand. Common.

▲ Striped Venus *Venus striatula* 3.5cm wide. Valves nearly triangular in shape, with close concentric ridges. Burrows on sandy shores. Common.

Other Seashore Creatures

► **Shrimp** *Crangon vulgaris*
6cm long. Hard segmented body.
5 pairs of walking legs, swimming
'legs' on abdomen. Long antennae.
Burrows in sand. Common.

◄ **Prawn** *Leander
serratus* 10cm long.
Hard, segmented body.
5 pairs walking legs, 2
with claws. Has spines
on horn between eyes
(lacking in shrimp).
Rock pools.

◄ **Acorn Barnacle**
Semibalanus balanoides
Up to 2cm wide. Body
concealed by 6 fused
plates. Legs protrude to
feed. Rocky shores.

► **Sea Slater** *Ligia
oceanica* Up to 3cm
long. Hard, segmented
oval, flattened body.
Active at night on high
tide line.

► **Sand Hopper**
Orchestia gammarella
Up to 2cm long. Red to
greenish-brown,
flattened sides. Under
stones or seaweed near
high tide line.

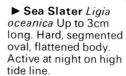

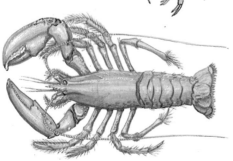

◄ **Lobster** *Homarus
vulgaris* 20–50cm long.
Stout, hard, segmented
body. Large pincers on
one pair of legs. Does
not swim but darts
backwards, using tail
and abdomen. Lives on
rocky coasts below tide
line.

► Dahlia Anemone
Tealia felina 5cm wide.
Tentacles thick, red or
pink, white bars. 'Body'
greyish-green,
patterned with red.
Rocky pools.

◄ Beadlet Anemone
Actinia equina 3cm
wide. Slender tentacles
with spots at base.
'Body' contracts to
conserve water when
tide is out. Rock pools.

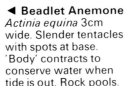

▲ Common Jellyfish
Aurelia aurita 30–40cm
wide. 4 long arms hang
from mouth. Common.

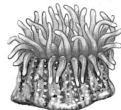

◄ Starfish *Asterias
rubens* Up to 40cm
wide. 5 pointed arms.
Mouth central, below.
Lives below tide line.
Common.

▲ Sea Urchin *Echinus
esculentus* 12cm wide.
Colour purple or red.
Sandy shores near low
tide mark.

► Ragworm *Nereis
diversicolor* Up to 10cm
long. Lives in burrows,
muddy shores.

► Lugworm *Arenicola
marina* 10–25cm long.
Front end thick, tail
thinner. Sandy shores
in 'U' shaped burrows.

◄ Hermit Crab
Eupagurus bernhardus
8–10cm long. Soft-
bodied. Lives in other
shells, moving house as
it grows. Common.

► Shore Crab
Carcinus maenas 5cm
long. 5 pairs of legs,
front pair with large
pincers. Walks
sideways. Common.

▲ Cuttlefish *Sepia
officinalis* Up to 50cm
long. Flat body with fin
around edge. Skeleton
(cuttle bone) often
found on shore.

101

Trees

Trees are plants which have become supremely successful in reaching up to the light and dominating all other forms of plant life. Light is essential to all green plants, as they need it to help in the manufacture of food. The tall trunk of a tree carries its leaves, where the food is manufactured, up into the light and the branches spread the leaves out to catch as much light as possible. Thus trees are the tallest living things, and in Britain some exceed 52 metres. The tallest tree in the world is the coast redwood of California, one of which reaches 113 metres.

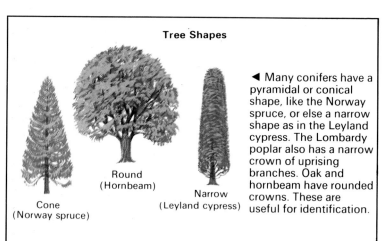

Tree Shapes

Cone
(Norway spruce)

Round
(Hornbeam)

Narrow
(Leyland cypress)

◀ Many conifers have a pyramidal or conical shape, like the Norway spruce, or else a narrow shape as in the Leyland cypress. The Lombardy poplar also has a narrow crown of uprising branches. Oak and hornbeam have rounded crowns. These are useful for identification.

There are two quite distinct groups of trees: conifers which bear their seeds in cones, and broadleaved trees with a variety of flowers and fruits. Conifers have simple needle-like or scale-like leaves which are thick and often waxy to avoid water loss. Most are evergreen and keep their leaves for several years. Broadleaved trees have larger, flatter leaves arranged carefully to catch the light. Most are thin and able to absorb and give off gases and water vapour easily while manufacturing food (photosynthesis), but cannot stand the rigorous conditions of winter. In northern Europe, many of them are deciduous, which means they drop their leaves in autumn. Broadleaved trees are sometimes called hardwoods because coniferous timber is more easily worked.

Simple unlobed

Hornbeam   Beech

Simple lobed

Common oak   Sycamore

Compound

Horse chestnut   Common ash

Leaf Shapes

Leaf shapes are very varied and the most useful characteristic for identification. Leaves of conifers are narrow, often sharp-pointed. They are very long and held in groups in pines. Scale-like leaves occur on cypresses and several other trees. Most other conifers have numerous needle-shaped leaves. Broadleaved trees have much more varied leaf shapes. Many have simple unlobed oval leaves. Some simple leaves are lobed regularly on each side like the oak, while many leaves have 3 to 5 radiating lobes like the maples. Compound leaves, divided into leaflets, fall into two groups: 'palmate' (hand-shaped) with about 5 lobes radiating from the tip of the leaf stalk and 'pinnate' with leaflets down either side of the stalk.

103

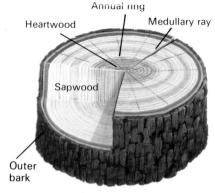

Heartwood
Annual ring
Medullary ray
Sapwood
Outer bark

▲ Section through tree trunk
The bark cracks as a new layer of wood is added each year. The cracks and fissures form distinctive patterns (see below).

The Tree Trunk

When a tree is felled, the structure of the stem can be seen and its age calculated. There are 'annual rings' of wood which have been added under the bark each year, made up of light-coloured spring wood and darker summer wood. This woody material gives the stem great strength. The outer rings conduct water up the tree. The wood in the centre, the 'heartwood', no longer carries water and is darker, but the annual rings can still be seen.

Different Types of Bark
Top row – deciduous   Bottom row – evergreen

English elm

London plane

Manna ash

Weymouth pine

Yew

Western hemlock

104

CONIFERS
Larches

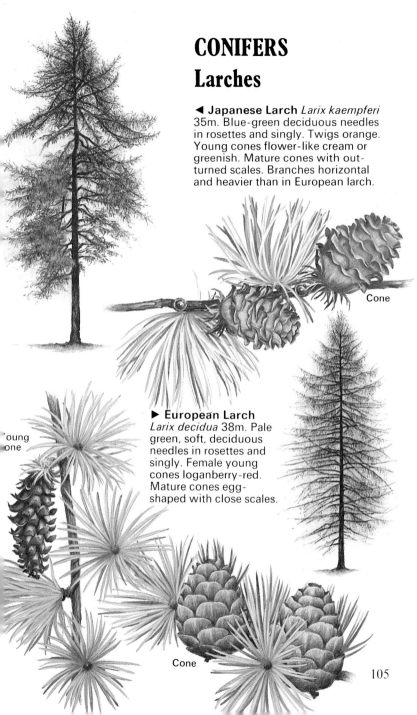

◀ **Japanese Larch** *Larix kaempferi*
35m. Blue-green deciduous needles
in rosettes and singly. Twigs orange.
Young cones flower-like cream or
greenish. Mature cones with out-
turned scales. Branches horizontal
and heavier than in European larch.

Cone

▶ **European Larch**
Larix decidua 38m. Pale
green, soft, deciduous
needles in rosettes and
singly. Female young
cones loganberry-red.
Mature cones egg-
shaped with close scales.

Young
one

Cone

105

Cedars and Firs

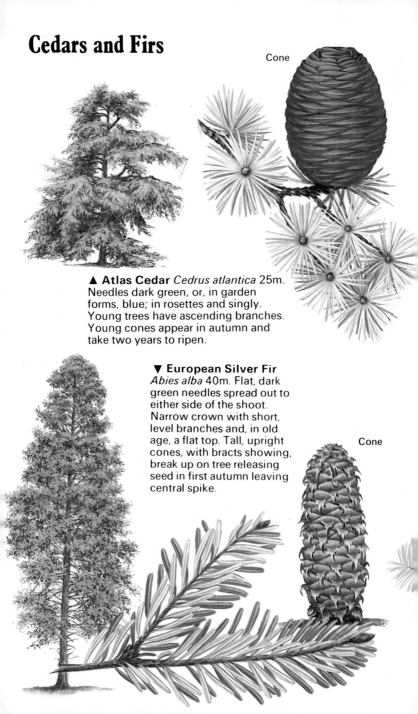

Cone

▲ **Atlas Cedar** *Cedrus atlantica* 25m.
Needles dark green, or, in garden
forms, blue; in rosettes and singly.
Young trees have ascending branches.
Young cones appear in autumn and
take two years to ripen.

▼ **European Silver Fir**
Abies alba 40m. Flat, dark
green needles spread out to
either side of the shoot.
Narrow crown with short,
level branches and, in old
age, a flat top. Tall, upright
cones, with bracts showing,
break up on tree releasing
seed in first autumn leaving
central spike.

Cone

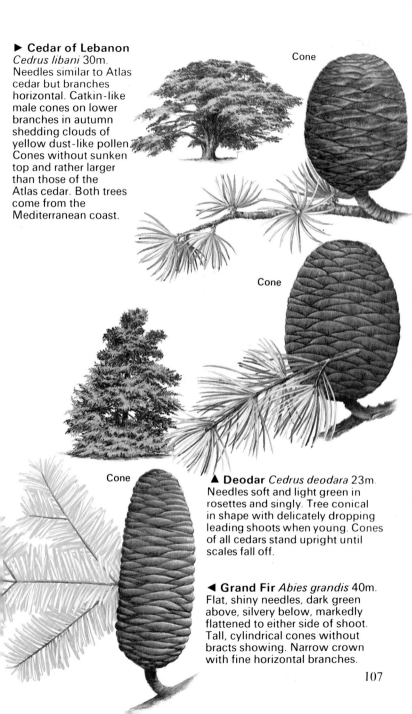

► **Cedar of Lebanon**
Cedrus libani 30m.
Needles similar to Atlas
cedar but branches
horizontal. Catkin-like
male cones on lower
branches in autumn
shedding clouds of
yellow dust-like pollen.
Cones without sunken
top and rather larger
than those of the
Atlas cedar. Both trees
come from the
Mediterranean coast.

Cone

Cone

Cone

▲ **Deodar** *Cedrus deodara* 23m.
Needles soft and light green in
rosettes and singly. Tree conical
in shape with delicately dropping
leading shoots when young. Cones
of all cedars stand upright until
scales fall off.

◄ **Grand Fir** *Abies grandis* 40m.
Flat, shiny needles, dark green
above, silvery below, markedly
flattened to either side of shoot.
Tall, cylindrical cones without
bracts showing. Narrow crown
with fine horizontal branches.

107

Hemlock and Douglas Fir

Cone

♀ flowers

♂ flowers

Cone

◄ **Western Hemlock**
Tsuga heterophylla
35m. Small, scattered,
flat needles of varying
lengths, dark green
above, two white bands
below. Small hanging
cones with rounded
scales turn from green
to brown and shake out
small black seeds. A
spire-like tree with a
broad base tapering to a
delicately drooping
leading shoot. Branch
ends also droop. A tree
from north western
America well suited to
Britain and growing to a
large size. It will
withstand dense shade
and grows well under
other trees.

◄ **Douglas Fir**
Pseudotsuga menziesii
60m. Needles flat and
soft, green above,
whitish below, parted
to show shoot above
and below. Bark
smooth with resin
blisters when young,
becoming corky. Buds
pointed, shiny brown,
like those of beech.
From north western
America and now the
tallest tree in Britain.

Spruces

Male cones with pollen

Mature cone

▲ **Norway Spruce** *Picea abies*
30m. Small sharp needles on pegs
which remain when they fall. Long,
cigar-shaped hanging cones with
rounded scales. A triangular tree
with regular branching, familiar as
the Christmas tree. Bark orange-
brown. Grows well in moist areas.

▼ **Sitka Spruce** *Picea sitchensis*
35m. Very sharp blue-green
needles on pegs. Bark flakes off.
Light brown hanging cones with
papery scales.

Cone

Pines

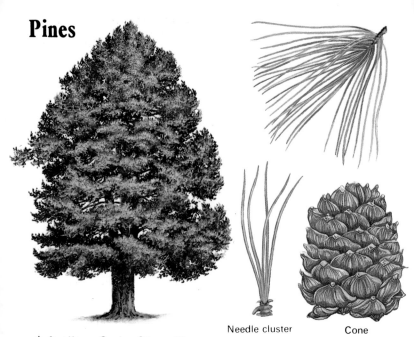

Needle cluster   Cone

▲ Arolla or Swiss Stone Pine
Pinus cembra 20m. Needles in
fives, stiff, giving foliage a dense
appearance. Crown of tree narrow
due to short, horizontal branches.
Small pointed buds. Egg-shaped
cones with thick cone scales and
fat, edible seeds that take $2\frac{1}{2}$ years
to ripen. The seeds are not shaken
out of the cone as in other pines
but the whole cone is shed when
the seeds are ripe.

▶ Monterey Pine *Pinus radiata*
30m. Needles in threes, grass-
green, soft. Has a broad crown
when old. Buds blunt pointed,
fairly large, sticky. Cones squat
with lop-sided base pressed hard
against them, usually in clusters of
three to five. Seed ripens in third
year but cones remain on tree
many years. Comes from a small
area on Californian coast and so
resistant to salt-laden winds.

Cone

110

◄ Scots Pine *Pinus sylvestris* 35m. Short, paired, blue-green needles. Young trees conical, old trees flat-topped with orange-red bark in crown. Remnants of natural forests in Scotland, spreading freely on sandy soils in the south. A good timber tree.

▼ Weymouth Pine *Pinus strobus* 35m. Thin needles closely held in bundles of five, bright bluish-green. Young trees conical, becoming a broad dome. Long cone with thin scales, often coated with white resin. From eastern America.

Cone

► Austrian and Corsican Pines *Pinus nigra* var. *nigra* and var. *maritima* 36m. Two varieties of the European black pine. Austrian has paired, coarse dark green needles. Corsican finer, grey-green needles. Austrian a tall, bushy tree common in shelter belts, particularly near sea as resistant to salt winds. Corsican an important plantation tree in eastern England. Both have branches in regular annual whorls. Buds large, onion-shaped. Young female cones red, paired at tips of shoots.

Cone

Cone

111

Redwoods

▶ **Giant Sequoia or
Wellingtonia**
*Sequoiadendron
giganteum* 50m. Small,
sharp, awl-like leaves
curve away from twig,
similar larger leaves
cover twig, both dark
green. Light brown
bark is thick, soft and
fibrous. Tall, regular,
spire-like tree, often
with lightning-struck
top. The descending
branches sweep up
at ends. A majestic
avenue tree from north
western America.

Cone

Autumn leaves

Cone

◀ **Dawn Redwood**
*Metasequoia
glyptostroboides* 20m.
Soft, flat, light green
leaves, very similar to
swamp cypress but
leaves and branchlets
oppositely arranged,
dropped in winter.
Buds arise below
branchlets. Young trees
pyramidal and regular
in outline. Bark fibrous,
orange-brown. Stalked
green cones rare.
Strikes easily from
cuttings. Known as a
fossil but discovered
growing in China in
1941 and introduced
widely since.

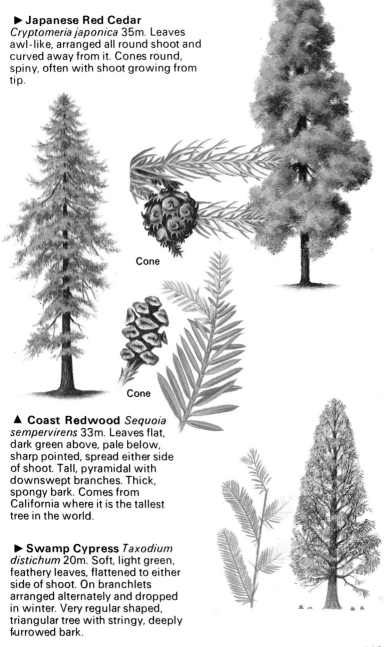

▶ Japanese Red Cedar

Cryptomeria japonica 35m. Leaves awl-like, arranged all round shoot and curved away from it. Cones round, spiny, often with shoot growing from tip.

Cone

Cone

▲ Coast Redwood *Sequoia sempervirens* 33m. Leaves flat, dark green above, pale below, sharp pointed, spread either side of shoot. Tall, pyramidal with downswept branches. Thick, spongy bark. Comes from California where it is the tallest tree in the world.

▶ Swamp Cypress *Taxodium distichum* 20m. Soft, light green, feathery leaves, flattened to either side of shoot. On branchlets arranged alternately and dropped in winter. Very regular shaped, triangular tree with stringy, deeply furrowed bark.

113

Cypresses

▶ **Lawson Cypress**
Chamaecyparis lawsoniana
25m. Leaves small, evergreen,
scale-like, in fours, one pair
larger than the other, with
white markings below.
Column-shaped, with dense
fine branches to ground. Stem
forked. Many small red male
cones on shoot-tips in spring.
Small brown cones with
hobnail-like scales.

Cone

Unripe cone

◀ **Leyland Cypress**
x *Cupressocyparis leylandii*
30m to date. Leaves
indistinguishable from
Lawson cypress but a dense
foliaged, broader, more
parallel sided crown, reaching
30m in 50 years. Seldom
cones, but strikes easily from
cuttings. Can be clipped hard
and, with its rapid growth, is
ideal for hedges.

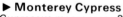

▶ **Monterey Cypress**
Cupressus macrocarpa 25m.
Leaves very small, scale-like,
pointing forwards, dark green
with pale margin. Column-
shaped when young with
dense foliage, becoming flat-
topped when old. Cones are
large, globular, purplish-
brown, with pronounced
knob on scales.

Unripe cone

114

▼ **Juniper** *Juniperus communis*
6m. Leaves needle-like, sharp, in threes around stem, blue-green with white bands on upper surface. Usually a densely foliaged, spreading bush. Seeds in purple berry-like cones on female trees.

Unripe cone

▲ **Italian Cypress** *Cupressus sempervirens* 15m. Small, scale-like, dark green leaves without points, closely pressed to stem giving a thread-like appearance. An upright, very narrow tree. Large, rounded cones like those of Monterey cypress with lumps on cone scales.

Cone

Cone

▲ ▶ **Western Red Cedar** *Thuja plicata* 30m. Scale-like leaves similar to Lawson cypress, in flat sprays with white patches on undersides. Conical with dense foliage and upright leading shoot. Bark cinnamon red, soft, peeling in long strips. Root buttresses at base of trunk. Cones have few thin, leaf-like scales.

115

Other Evergreens

▶ Chile Pine or Monkey Puzzle
Araucaria araucana
25m. Leaves are large, stiff and thick with sharp points, dark green, growing all round shoot. Branches in distinct annual whorls until old and flat-topped with bare trunk. Bark grey and roughened by persistent leaf bases. Female cones large, golden shiny globes on separate trees. Seeds large and edible.

Cone

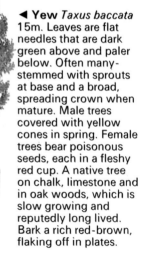

◀ Yew *Taxus baccata*
15m. Leaves are flat needles that are dark green above and paler below. Often many-stemmed with sprouts at base and a broad, spreading crown when mature. Male trees covered with yellow cones in spring. Female trees bear poisonous seeds, each in a fleshy red cup. A native tree on chalk, limestone and in oak woods, which is slow growing and reputedly long lived. Bark a rich red-brown, flaking off in plates.

Palms

► **Chusan Palm** *Trachycarpus fortunei* 11 m. Fan-shaped leaves with long stalks, divided into about 30 long, narrow segments, crowded at top of shaggy stem. Grown only in south and west of Britain.

▼ **European (Dwarf) Fan Palm** *Chamaerops humilis* 4m. Fan-shaped leaves with long stalks and 12–15 segments. Growing naturally in Mediterranean, does not form a stem, but in cultivation produces a fibrous trunk of several metres clothed with old leaf bases. Occasionally grown in southern Britain.

BROADLEAVED TREES
Poplars and Willows

Winter

◄ ▶ White Poplar *Populus alba* 20m. Leaves alternate, lobed, dark green above, white below. Buds white and hairy. Upper bark white with large, diamond-shaped markings. Open, rounded crown.

▶ Lombardy Poplar *Populus nigra* var. *italica* 28m. Leaves alternate, triangular, pointed, with small, regular teeth. Glossy green above with translucent margin, paler below. Narrow crown with close, upright branches and fluted trunk. A natural variation of black poplar.

Summer leaves

♀ catkins

◄ Aspen *Populus tremula* 20m. Leaves alternate, round, thin with wavy margin on flattened leaf stalk which causes them to flutter. A small, conical tree with light, open branches. Bark diamond-marked. Occurs in groups.

Autumn leaf

Winter

◄ Black Italian Poplar
Populus x *euramericana* var. *serotina* 40m. Leaves alternate, triangular, emerge bronze and turn a light, fresh green. Leaf stalk flattened. A large, open crown with some heavy, upswept branches, stem straight and clear of branches. One of the many hybrids resulting from crosses between European and American black poplars.

► White Willow *Salix alba*
20m. Leaves alternate, long, pointed, with regular teeth, grey-green above, dense white hairs below. Ascending branches form narrow crown. The bark is a network of ridges. Male and female flowers are green catkins on separate trees. One of the common weeping willows, 'Chrysocoma' is a white willow.

♀ catkin

♀ catkins

◄ Crack Willow *Salix fragilis* 15m. Leaves alternate, very long and narrow, bright, glossy green above, grey below, not hairy. Broad open crown with hanging branches. Orange twigs snap easily. Grows near water. Branches are often cut back to trunk.

119

Willow and Hazel

► **Goat Willow** *Salix caprea*
7m. Leaves alternate, oval
with a rounded base, a short
point at tip and wavy margin.
Dark green above, dense grey
hairs below, leathery. Leaf
stalk also hairy. Large,
pointed, bright red buds in
winter. A small bushy tree
with rounded crown. Twigs
thick and knobbly. The true
'pussy willow' – with
rounded male catkins covered
in grey, silky hairs and yellow
pollen when ripe. Female
flowers similar, turning green.
Common on waste ground
and scrub woodland.

♀ catkins

♀ flowers

♂ catkins

♂ catkins

Autumn leaf

Ripe nut

◄ **Hazel** *Corylus avellana* 12m.
Leaves alternate, rounded with
stiff hairs. Long male catkins
(lamb's tails) open yellow from
December. Female flowers a tight
bud with only two scarlet styles
protruding. Nuts in green leafy
bracts. Usually a many-stemmed
bush; occasionally a small tree.
Frequently coppiced. Common.

Alder and Birch

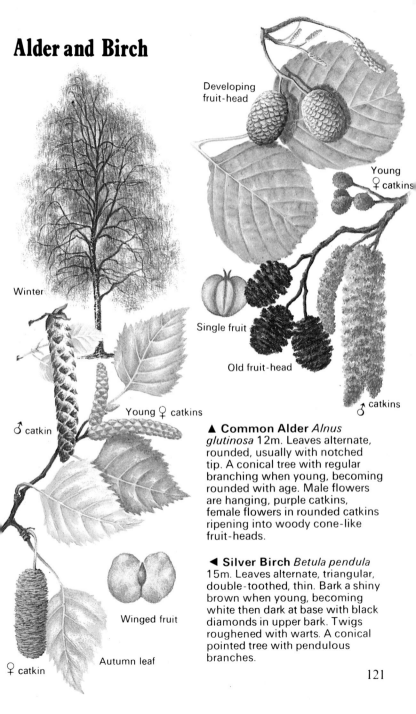

Developing fruit-head

Young ♀ catkins

Winter

Single fruit

Old fruit-head

♂ catkins

♂ catkin

Young ♀ catkins

▲ **Common Alder** *Alnus glutinosa* 12m. Leaves alternate, rounded, usually with notched tip. A conical tree with regular branching when young, becoming rounded with age. Male flowers are hanging, purple catkins, female flowers in rounded catkins ripening into woody cone-like fruit-heads.

◀ **Silver Birch** *Betula pendula* 15m. Leaves alternate, triangular, double-toothed, thin. Bark a shiny brown when young, becoming white then dark at base with black diamonds in upper bark. Twigs roughened with warts. A conical pointed tree with pendulous branches.

Winged fruit

♀ catkin

Autumn leaf

121

Hornbeam and Beech

► **Hornbeam**
Carpinus betulus 10m.
Leaves alternate, oval,
double-toothed with 15
pairs of pronounced
parallel veins. A small,
bushy tree with a broad
crown and fluted trunk.
Bark silvery-grey, only
occasionally fissured.
Female catkins a leafy
green, appearing with
leaves, ripening to
hanging bunches of
3-pronged bracts
holding brown nutlets.
Only in southern
England. Often
pollarded.

♂ catkin

Fruit

Winter

Winter twig

▼ **Beech** *Fagus sylvatica* 25m. Leaves
alternate, oval with wavy margin. Light
green at first, darkening as
summer proceeds. A tall slender
tree with a few branches
in woodlands, heavy, spreading
branches in open land. Bark smooth,
grey, becoming only slightly fissured
in some trees. Nuts enclosed in
spiky 4-valved husks.

Autumn

Ripe nut in husk

Winter bud

122

Chestnut and Oak

▼ Sweet Chestnut
Castanea sativa 25m. Leaves
alternate, long, toothed with
prominent parallel veins.
Spreading branches form a
massive crown. Flowers mid-
summer, fruits in spiny cupule.

Summer and
autumn leaves

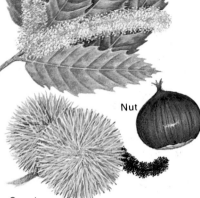

Nut

Cupule

Winter

▼ Holm Oak *Quercus ilex* 20m.
Alternate evergreen leaves, narrow,
dark green above, buff or white below.
Young leaves on lower part of tree
often sharp-toothed, resembling holly
leaves. A rounded, dense crown, often
with more than one stem. The small
acorn is half enclosed in a fawn-
coloured cup with felted scales.
Mediterranean tree popular in Britain.

Ripening
acorns

Oaks

◀ **Sessile Oak** *Quercus petraea* 21m. Leaves alternate, lobed with veins running to the tips of the lobes. Leaves stalked, acorns stalkless and rounded at tip. Crown fan-shaped with upswept branches arising at different levels on the trunk. Occurs naturally on light soils and in upland western Britain.

▶ ▼ **Common Oak** *Quercus robur* 23m. Leaves alternate, rounded lobes with veins to lobes and to indentations. 'Ears' at base of leaf either side of very short leaf stalk. Acorns on long stalks, tall and parallel-sided, usually paired. Rounded crown with short bole. Occurs on lime-rich loams and clays.

Winter

◄ **Cork Oak** *Quercus suber* 16m. Alternate, evergreen leaves with wavy margins and very shallow, spine-tipped lobes; dark green above, grey below. A low, spreading crown with twisted trunk and branches. Bark grey, thick and corky, deeply fissued. Acorn cup has wavy margin and only loosely holds acorn. From southern Europe, only in parks and gardens in Britain. Outer bark periodically stripped for cork manufacture in southern Europe.

▼ **Turkey Oak** *Quercus cerris* 25m. Leaves alternate, dark green and shiny above, hairy below, deeply and regularly lobed with paired stipules at base. Buds whiskered. The tall, narrow acorn which takes two years to ripen is set deeply in a stalkless 'mossy' cup covered with long, pointed scales. A tall, fast-growing tree with uprising branches forming a wide crown.

♂ catkins

♀ flower

125

Maples and Plane

▼ ► **Norway Maple** *Acer
platanoides* 15m. Leaves
opposite, fan-shaped with 5
sharply-pointed lobes. Thin,
shiny, bright green. Bud scales
brown. A medium-sized tree
with an open regular crown,
less dense than sycamore.
Fruits in pairs at a wide angle.

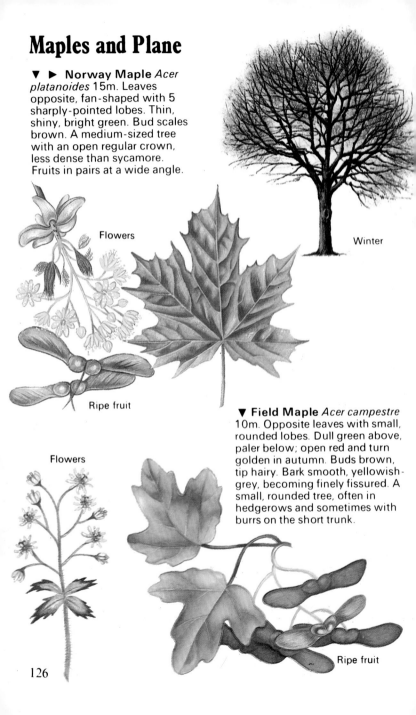

Flowers

Winter

Ripe fruit

Flowers

▼ **Field Maple** *Acer campestre*
10m. Opposite leaves with small,
rounded lobes. Dull green above,
paler below; open red and turn
golden in autumn. Buds brown,
tip hairy. Bark smooth, yellowish-
grey, becoming finely fissured. A
small, rounded tree, often in
hedgerows and sometimes with
burrs on the short trunk.

Ripe fruit

Flowers

Fruit

Winter

▲ **Sycamore** *Acer pseudoplatanus* 20m. Large, opposite leaves with 5-pointed lobes, dark green, leathery. Large green buds. A large tree with a dense, spreading crown. Paired fruit wings, closely angled. Seeds freely all over Britain and grows well, even in exposed places.

▶ **London Plane** *Platanus x hybrida* 30m. 5-lobed leaves like a maple but alternate and bright green. Smooth, grey bark flakes off to leave yellow patches. A tall tree with a clean stem and large spreading branches forming a broad crown. Round, spiky bobble-like fruits hang on long stalks all winter. A hybrid between oriental and American plane which arose naturally and has proved ideal for city use, so a common street and park tree.

♀flowers

♂ flowers

Winter

Fruit cluster

127

Horse Chestnut and Limes

Opening bud

▼ Horse Chestnut *Aesculus hippocastanum* 25m. Opposite, hand-shaped, dark green leaves with 5 to 7 stalkless leaflets, narrow at base and broadening to tip. Large sticky buds. Rich brown seeds (conkers) in spiny green case. Short trunk with few heavy branches upturned at the ends.

Fruit opening to show conker

Fruit

Winter

▲ ▶ Common Lime *Tilia x europaea* 25m. Alternate, heart-shaped leaves with tufts of hairs in vein axils below. Buds red-brown with one large and one small scale. Round ribbed fruits hang from leafy wing. Domed crown with arching branches.

▶ Small-leaved Lime *Tilia cordata* 20m. The heart-shaped leaf is nearly round and has orange hairs in vein axils below. Buds lop-sided. A tall domed tree with arching branches. Sprouts and burrs common at base of trunk. Popular avenue tree.

Winter

Fruit

Elms

Flowers

Ripening fruit

Winter

Fruit

Winter twig

▶ Wych Elm *Ulmus glabra*
20m. Leaves alternate, oval,
large, unequal base with one
side covering stalk. Dark
green, rough. Buds large and
hairy. Broad, rounded crown.
Seed in centre of round,
winged fruit.

Winter

▲ English Elm *Ulmus procera* 30m.
Small, alternate leaves with lop-sided
base. Dark green, rough and hairy.
Buds small. A tall domed tree with few
large branches. Suckers freely and
often several hedgerow trees are
connected by common root system.
Common in southern England before
Dutch elm disease.

Fruit

Flowers

Ash and Walnut

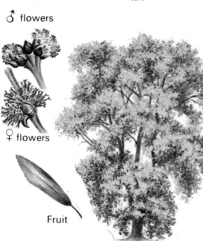

♂ flowers

♀ flowers

Fruit

◄ **Ash** *Fraxinus excelsior*
25m. Opposite leaves divided
into 9 to 13 toothed leaflets
on short stalks, terminal
leaflet longer-stalked. Comes
into leaf late, after the
bunches of purplish hanging
flowers. Buds large, black,
shaped like a bishop's mitre.
Bark grey becoming shallowly
fissured. A tall tree with
sparse ascending branches
forming an open crown
casting little shade. Fruits
hang in clusters on tree
throughout winter.

► **Manna Ash** *Fraxinus
ornus* 20m. Opposite leaves
divided into 5 to 9 leaflets on
short stalks, hairs on
underside beside veins. Buds
brown. Creamy-white flowers
borne in dense heads in June
when the tree is in full leaf.

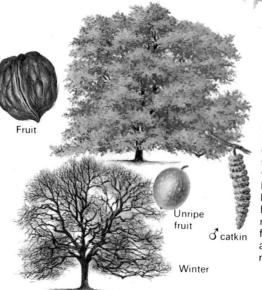

Fruit

Unripe
fruit

♂ catkin

Winter

◄ **Walnut** *Juglans
regia* 15m. Alternate
leaves with 7 to 9
leaflets with short
stalks, terminal leaflet
the largest with long
stalk. Emerge bronze in
spring and turn light
green. A broad
spreading open crown
with few twisted
branches. Twigs cut
longitudinally show
hollow pith with cross
membranes. Green
fruits attract squirrels
and do not always
ripen.

Rose Family

▶ Hawthorn

Crataegus monogyna
8m. Leaves alternate
with 3 to 7 rounded
lobes, dark green with
leafy stipules at base of
leaf stalk. Twigs have
sharp thorns. Bole
fluted and furrowed. A
small much-branched
tree with rounded
crown. White, scented
flowers in May turn to
dark red haw berries in
autumn which attract
birds.

▼ Rowan *Sorbus*

aucuparia 7m.
Alternate leaves of 9 to
15 stalkless leaflets
with forward-pointing
teeth. Large, hairy, oval
buds. Smooth grey
bark with orange
breathing pores. A
small, slender tree with
few ascending
branches and narrow
crown. In May, cream-
white flowers, in late
summer, red berries
attract birds.

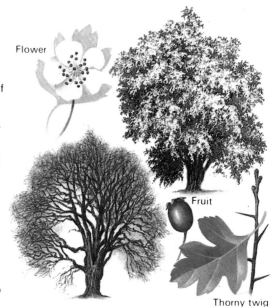

Flower

Fruit

Winter

Thorny twig

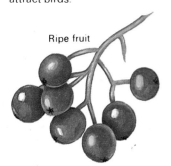

Ripe fruit

Winter

131

Rose Family

Flowers

Ripe fruit

▲ **Whitebeam** *Sorbus aria* 8m.
Alternate oval leaves, double-
toothed; green above, felted with
white hairs below. Bud also hairy.
A small, compact crown formed of
upswept branches on a short stem.
Bark is smooth, pale grey. Creamy-
white sweet-scented flowers in
May. Scarlet berries attract birds.

▼ **Crab Apple** *Malus sylvestris*
10m. Leaves alternate, long to
oval, toothed with white hairs on
undersides. A broad-crowned
tree or shrub, often leaning. Large
pinkish-white flowers. The green
apple only turns partly red when
ripe and is bitter. In hedgerows
and copses.

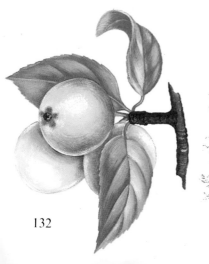

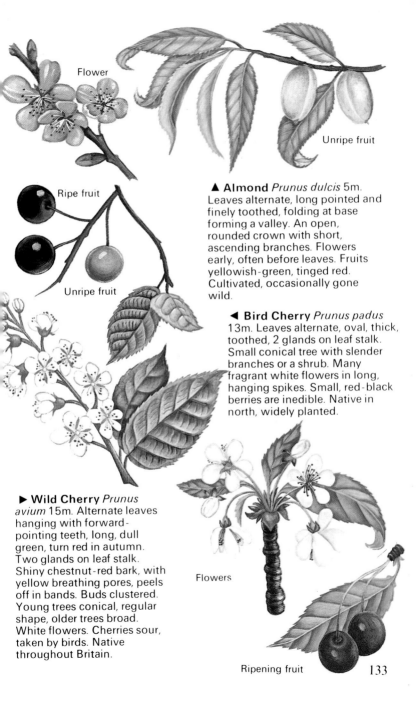

Flower

Unripe fruit

Ripe fruit

Unripe fruit

▲ **Almond** *Prunus dulcis* 5m.
Leaves alternate, long pointed and
finely toothed, folding at base
forming a valley. An open,
rounded crown with short,
ascending branches. Flowers
early, often before leaves. Fruits
yellowish-green, tinged red.
Cultivated, occasionally gone
wild.

◀ **Bird Cherry** *Prunus padus*
13m. Leaves alternate, oval, thick,
toothed, 2 glands on leaf stalk.
Small conical tree with slender
branches or a shrub. Many
fragrant white flowers in long,
hanging spikes. Small, red-black
berries are inedible. Native in
north, widely planted.

▶ **Wild Cherry** *Prunus
avium* 15m. Alternate leaves
hanging with forward-
pointing teeth, long, dull
green, turn red in autumn.
Two glands on leaf stalk.
Shiny chestnut-red bark, with
yellow breathing pores, peels
off in bands. Buds clustered.
Young trees conical, regular
shape, older trees broad.
White flowers. Cherries sour,
taken by birds. Native
throughout Britain.

Flowers

Ripening fruit

133

Pea Family

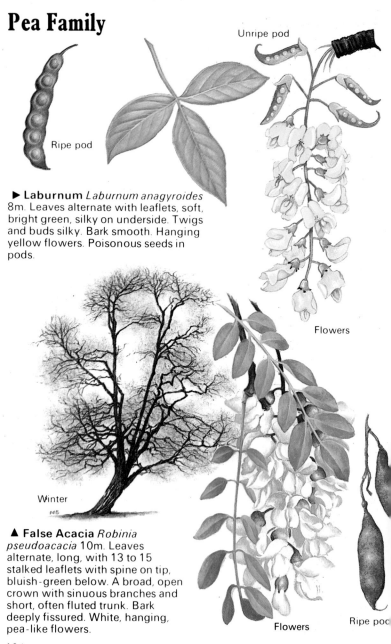

Ripe pod

Unripe pod

Flowers

► **Laburnum** *Laburnum anagyroides*
8m. Leaves alternate with leaflets, soft,
bright green, silky on underside. Twigs
and buds silky. Bark smooth. Hanging
yellow flowers. Poisonous seeds in
pods.

Winter

▲ **False Acacia** *Robinia
pseudoacacia* 10m. Leaves
alternate, long, with 13 to 15
stalked leaflets with spine on tip,
bluish-green below. A broad, open
crown with sinuous branches and
short, often fluted trunk. Bark
deeply fissured. White, hanging,
pea-like flowers.

Flowers

Ripe pod

Elder, Holly and Olive

► **Elder** *Sambucus nigra* 9m. Leaves opposite with 5 to 7 leaflets, margins toothed. More often a bush than a tree. Light brown corky bark. Heads of numerous, creamy-white flowers with a heavy, sweet smell. Common on rough ground.

Ripe fruit

◄ **Holly** *Ilex aquifolium* 10m. Alternate, thick, shiny evergreen leaves with sharp spines. Bark smooth, green at first, warty and silver-grey later. Separate male and female trees. Flowers on both are small, clustered and greenish-white. Dense bunches of red berries occur on female trees. Common everywhere.

► **Olive** *Olea europaea* 10m. Long, opposite evergreen leaves, silvery-grey. A small, rounded tree with twisted branches and trunk. Small white flowers. Few trees flower in Britain. The rounded fleshy green fruit is oily; it ripens black and is edible. Mediterranean. Only planted in southern Britain, where fruit does not ripen.

Unripe fruit

Ripe fruit

Wild Flowers

Flowers are separated into families by their structure, which can be complicated and highly specialized. The flowers in the buttercup family *Ranunculaceae* are examples of the simplest type. An outer ring of greenish-yellow sepals surrounds the bright yellow petals, which are all similar in size and shape. The flower contains both male and female parts. The male parts are the numerous stamens with anthers bearing pollen, the female, the many ovaries each with a style and stigma. Such a flower is called a regular, perfect flower. In contrast, some flowers have sepals which are highly coloured and indistinguishable from the petals. Sepals and petals may be joined at the base, forming tubes.

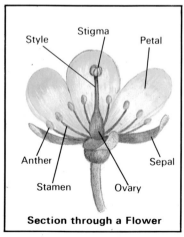

Section through a Flower

External Features of a Flowering Plant

Flower
Flower stalk
Bract
Leaf
Leaf stalk
Leaf axil
Stipule
Stem
Root

Style
Stigma
Petal
Anther
Stamen
Ovary
Sepal

As well as living in particular conditions, each plant often grows together with other species. Such associations of plants are called 'plant communities', and are typical of a particular climate and kind of soil. Some plants are short-lived (annuals and ephemerals), some take two years to mature (biennials), while others persist for many years, flowering every year (perennials).

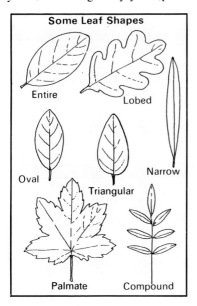

Some Leaf Shapes

Entire

Lobed

Oval

Narrow

Triangular

Palmate

Compound

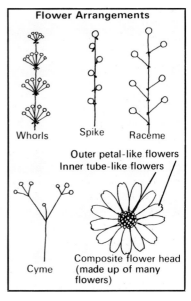

Flower Arrangements

Whorls

Spike

Raceme

Outer petal-like flowers
Inner tube-like flowers

Cyme

Composite flower head (made up of many flowers)

CLUES AND HINTS

Where to look: Wild flowers are everywhere, in towns as well as in the countryside.

Collecting flowers: Never dig up wild flowers, and do not pick a flower if you can only see a few of its kind. It might be very rare. You can pick the commoner flowers and press them, keeping a record of when and where found, the kind of soil and the height of the plant.

Leaf shape (see above): Look carefully at the shape of the leaf, whether it is entire or lobed, and its veining, as well as the way the leaves are arranged on the stem.

Flower arrangement (see above): Count the number of petals and notice the arrangement of flowers on the stem, whether solitary or in whorls, spikes, racemes, cymes or composite heads.

Buttercups

▶ **Meadow Buttercup** *Ranunculus acris* Up to 100cm. 5 bright, glossy, yellow, rounded petals, 5 green sepals. Common in grassland. Flowers April to October.

▲ **Lesser Spearwort** *Ranunculus flammula* 8–50cm. Leaves oval or long and narrow. Stem thick. 5 small petals. Common in wet places. Flowers May to September.

▶ **Lesser Celandine** *Ranunculus ficaria* 10–25cm. Single flowers on stem, 8 to 12 bright yellow petals, long and narrow. Leaves spade-shaped. Woods and hedge banks. Flowers early spring.

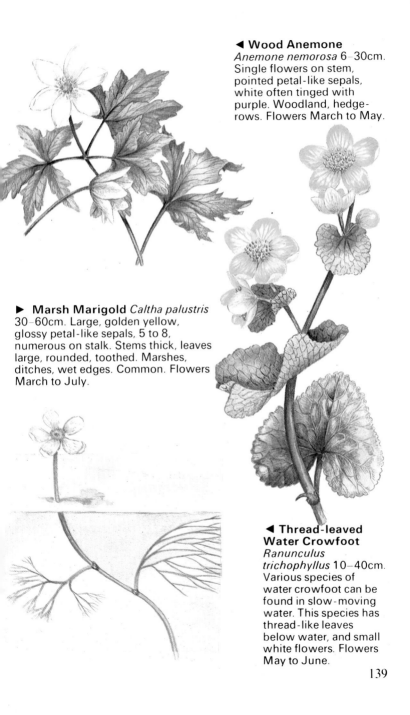

◄ Wood Anemone
Anemone nemorosa 6–30cm. Single flowers on stem, pointed petal-like sepals, white often tinged with purple. Woodland, hedgerows. Flowers March to May.

► Marsh Marigold *Caltha palustris*
30–60cm. Large, golden yellow, glossy petal-like sepals, 5 to 8, numerous on stalk. Stems thick, leaves large, rounded, toothed. Marshes, ditches, wet edges. Common. Flowers March to July.

◄ Thread-leaved Water Crowfoot
Ranunculus trichophyllus 10–40cm. Various species of water crowfoot can be found in slow-moving water. This species has thread-like leaves below water, and small white flowers. Flowers May to June.

139

Poppies and Water-lilies

◄ Greater Celandine
Chelidonium majus
30–90cm. Poisonous
bright orange juice in
broken stem. Long seed
pods. Leaves with
toothed leaflets.
Common. Hedgerows,
walls. Flowers May to
August.

Seed capsule

Flower bud

► Field Poppy
Papaver rhoeas 20–
60cm. White juice in
broken stem. Stem
hairy. 4 large, bright red
petals fall quickly after
flowering. Abundant
where weedkiller not
used, corn fields, waste
places. Flowers June to
August. Annual.

▼ Yellow Water-lily
Nuphar lutea Leaves up
to 30cm wide. Large,
spade-shaped, fleshy
leaves float on surface
of ponds and lakes.
Flowers June to
August.

▼ White Water-lily
Nymphaea alba Leaves
up to 30cm wide.
Large, circular fleshy
leaves float on water.
Numerous pointed
white petals. Flowers
June to September.

Fumitory and Cabbage Family

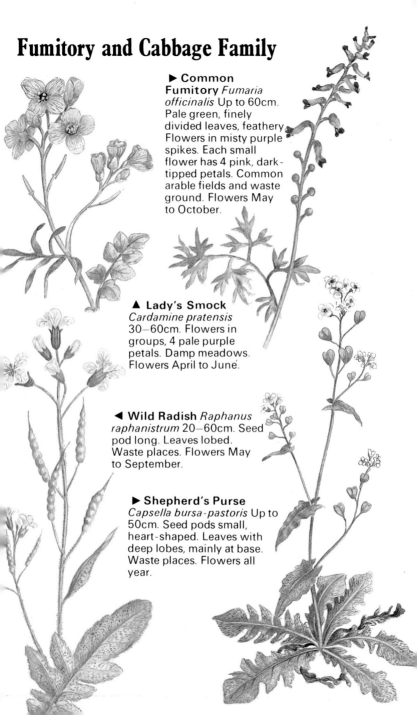

▶ **Common Fumitory** *Fumaria officinalis* Up to 60cm. Pale green, finely divided leaves, feathery. Flowers in misty purple spikes. Each small flower has 4 pink, dark-tipped petals. Common arable fields and waste ground. Flowers May to October.

▲ **Lady's Smock** *Cardamine pratensis* 30–60cm. Flowers in groups, 4 pale purple petals. Damp meadows. Flowers April to June.

◀ **Wild Radish** *Raphanus raphanistrum* 20–60cm. Seed pod long. Leaves lobed. Waste places. Flowers May to September.

▶ **Shepherd's Purse** *Capsella bursa-pastoris* Up to 50cm. Seed pods small, heart-shaped. Leaves with deep lobes, mainly at base. Waste places. Flowers all year.

Violets, Milkwort and St John's Wort

▼ **Sweet Violet** *Viola odorata* 5–10cm. Flowers sweet-scented. 5 petals, the lowest with a pouch-like spur at base. Leaves rounded, heart-shaped. Hedge banks. Flowers February to April.

Seed capsule

White form

▲ **Wild Pansy** *Viola tricolor* 10–30cm. Upper petals purple, lower yellow with dark lines. Several flowers on a stem. Cultivated and grassy places. Flowers April to September.

▼ **Common Milkwort** *Polygala vulgaris* 10–30cm. Weak spreading stems. Small, flat flowers, blue, pink or white. Grassland. Flowers May to September.

► **Common St John's Wort** *Hypericum perforatum* 30–90cm. Flower pale yellow, 5 petals with black dots on edges. Leaves opposite, dotted with glands. Stalk woody with raised lines. Common in grassland, hedgerows. Flowers June to September.

Stitchworts

▶ **Red Campion** *Silene dioica* 30–90cm. Leaves opposite, pointed and hairy. The 5 petals are heart-shaped at end. The green sepals form a ridged tube with 5 teeth at top. 10 stamens. Shady, damp woods and hedge banks. Flowers May to June.

Flower

◀ **Ragged Robin** *Lychnis flos-cuculi* 30–75cm. Leaves opposite. 5 pale pink petals, deeply divided into four. Sepals form a tube. 10 stamens. Wet meadows. Flowers May to June.

▶ **Common Mouse-ear Chickweed** *Cerastium holosteoides* 45cm. Leaves small, oval, very hairy. Flowers have 5 white petals with heart-shaped ends. Sepals only a little shorter than petals. Waste places. Flowers April to September.

143

Stitchworts

◀ **Greater Stitchwort** *Stellaria holostea* 15—60cm. Weak, slender stem with 4 sides. 5 white, heart-shaped petals. Common in woods, hedgerows. Flowers April to June.

▶ **Corn Spurrey** *Spergula arvensis* 7—40cm. Trailing stems, leaves long and thread-like. Stem and leaves sticky due to hairs. Cornfields and waste places. Flowers June to August.

▶ **Common Chickweed** *Stellaria media* 5—40cm. Straggling leafy stems. 5 deeply divided white petals. Reddish stamens. Common gardens and waste places. Flowers all year.

Goosefoot, Mallow and Wood Sorrel

◀ **Fat Hen**
Chenopodium album
30–50cm. This member
of the goosefoot family
has numerous small,
green flowers in dense
bunches. Leaves
toothed and thick with
hairs giving the plant a
'mealy' appearance.
Waste places. Common.
Flowers July to
October.

▼ **Common Mallow** *Malva
sylvestris* 45–90cm. 5 purple
or white petals with darker
stripes. Heart-shaped at tip,
narrowing to base. Leaves
hairy with 5 to 7 triangular-
shaped lobes. Common on
roadsides. Flowers June to
September.

Flower

◀ **Wood Sorrel** *Oxalis
acetosella* 10–15cm. Leaves
clover-like on long slender
stalks. Single flower on stem,
with 5 rounded petals. Woods
especially oak and beech, in
shade. Flowers April to May.

145

Geraniums and Balsam

► **Meadow Cranesbill**
Geranium pratense 30–40cm.
Blue flowers have 5 petals
with rounded ends. Fruits
have long pointed ends from
which the name comes.
Flowers June to September.

◄ **Herb Robert** *Geranium
robertianum* 10–50cm. Stem often
red, hairy. Plant has a characteristic
musty smell. 5 pinkish petals. Stamens
coloured orange by pollen. Fruits have
thin beak. Common. Hedgerows and
woodland. Flowers May to September.

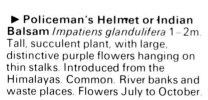

► **Policeman's Helmet or Indian
Balsam** *Impatiens glandulifera* 1–2m.
Tall, succulent plant, with large,
distinctive purple flowers hanging on
thin stalks. Introduced from the
Himalayas. Common. River banks and
waste places. Flowers July to October.

146

Pea Family

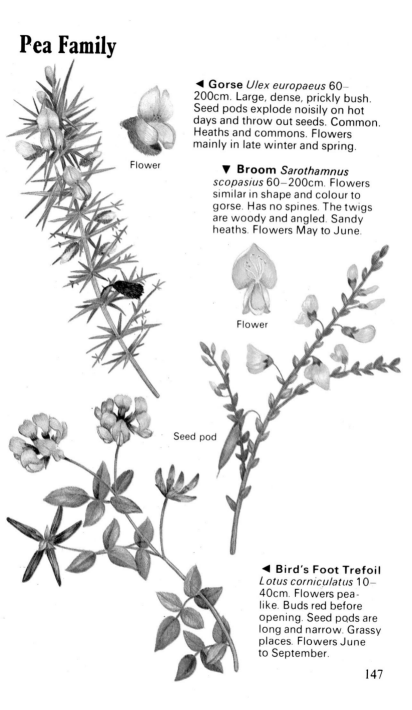

◄ **Gorse** *Ulex europaeus* 60–200cm. Large, dense, prickly bush. Seed pods explode noisily on hot days and throw out seeds. Common. Heaths and commons. Flowers mainly in late winter and spring.

Flower

▼ **Broom** *Sarothamnus scopasius* 60–200cm. Flowers similar in shape and colour to gorse. Has no spines. The twigs are woody and angled. Sandy heaths. Flowers May to June.

Flower

Seed pod

◄ **Bird's Foot Trefoil** *Lotus corniculatus* 10–40cm. Flowers pea-like. Buds red before opening. Seed pods are long and narrow. Grassy places. Flowers June to September.

147

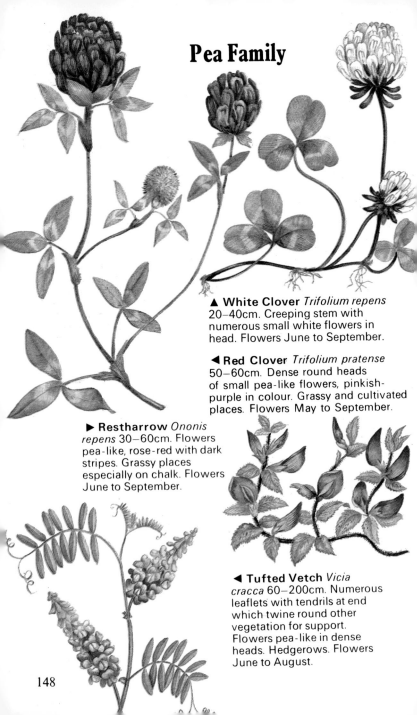

Pea Family

▲ **White Clover** *Trifolium repens*
20–40cm. Creeping stem with
numerous small white flowers in
head. Flowers June to September.

◀ **Red Clover** *Trifolium pratense*
50–60cm. Dense round heads
of small pea-like flowers, pinkish-
purple in colour. Grassy and cultivated
places. Flowers May to September.

▶ **Restharrow** *Ononis
repens* 30–60cm. Flowers
pea-like, rose-red with dark
stripes. Grassy places
especially on chalk. Flowers
June to September.

◀ **Tufted Vetch** *Vicia
cracca* 60–200cm. Numerous
leaflets with tendrils at end
which twine round other
vegetation for support.
Flowers pea-like in dense
heads. Hedgerows. Flowers
June to August.

148

Rose Family

◀ **Dog Rose** *Rosa canina* 1–3m. Long arching stems with many long, curved, sharp prickles. Leaves have 4 to 6 toothed leaflets; with leafy stipules attached to base of leaf stalk. Flowers showy, large with five heart-shaped pinkish petals which fall quickly. Numerous yellow stamens. The 5 green sepals turn back after flowering and fall before the fruit (round red, fleshy 'hip') is ripe. Flowers in hedgerows, June to July. Many other species of wild rose can be found growing in hedgerows and scrub.

▼ **Wild Strawberry** *Fragaria vesca* 5–30cm. Leaves are in tufts. Long runners are produced which root and form new plants. Woodland. Flowers April to July.

▲ **Bramble** *Rubus fruticosus* Long, rambling, woody stems with thorns. Flowers are white or tinged with pink. The 5 petals are separated from each other. 5 pointed sepals, often turned back. Fruit is the well-known blackberry. Hedgerows, woods. Flowers May to September.

◄ **Meadowsweet** *Filipendula ulmaria* 60–120cm. Creamy-white heads of small flowers. Leaves, 5 to 9 leaflets, covered with whitish hairs below. Reddish stems. Marshes and wet grassland. Flowers June to September.

Rose Family and Stonecrop

▶ **Water Avens** *Geum rivale* 20–60cm. The nodding flowers have 5 long sepals alternating with 5 shorter ones. 5 pinkish-orange petals and numerous yellow stamens. Leaves 7 to 13 leaflets, the end one rounded, lobed and toothed. Marshy places. Flowers May to September. Wood avens *Geum urbanum* similar to water avens but with yellow flowers.

Flower

◀ **Silverweed** *Potentilla anserina* Up to 80cm. Leaves in rosettes on long runners which root at intervals. Green above, covered with dense, silvery-white hairs below. Flower has long, often red stalk. 5 round yellow petals. Waste places. Flowers June to August. Another species, tormentil *Potentilla erecta*, has yellow flowers with 4 petals.

▶ **Biting Stonecrop** *Sedum acre* 2–10cm. Small, round, fleshy leaves crowded together, often forming dense mats. Flowers bright yellow. Walls, dry grassland. Flowers June to July.

151

Saxifrage, Grass of Parnassus, Loosestrife and Sundew

◀ **Rue-leaved Saxifrage**
Saxifraga tridactylites 2–15cm. Small white flowers with 5 petals. Leaves grow from rosette at ground level. Dry places. Flowers April to June.

▶ **Grass of Parnassus** *Parnassia palustris* 10–30cm. Large, single white flower with 5 rounded, green-veined petals. Wet meadows, uplands. Flowers July to October.

◀ **Purple Loosestrife**
Lythrum salicaria 60–120cm. Flowers in whorls on dense, long, purple spikes. Margins of lakes and ponds. Flowers June to August.

▶ **Sundew** *Drosera rotundifolia* 6–25cm. Rosettes of round leaves covered with red sticky glands for catching flies. Bogs, wet places. Flowers June to August.

Willowherbs and Ivy

Flower

◀ **Enchanter's Nightshade** *Circaea lutetiana* 30–60cm. Flowers in loose heads, 2 pinkish-white, lobed petals. Fruit has hooked hairs attaching it to the fur or hair of animals. Moist and shady woods, waste ground. Flowers June to August.

▶ **Rosebay Willowherb** *Epilobium angustifolium* Up to 120cm. Leaves long, narrow with raised mid vein. Flowers in long spikes tapering to point. Woolly seeds. Bare ground. Flowers July to September.

Flower

Seeds

Fruit cluster

◀ **Ivy** *Hedera helix* Climbs to 30m. Long, trailing woody stems. Clings to walls and trees and also creeps on ground. Evergreen. Flowers September to November.

153

Carrot Family

► **Cow Parsley** *Anthriscus sylvestris*
Up to 100cm. Flowers in umbels.
Hedgerows. Flowers April to June.

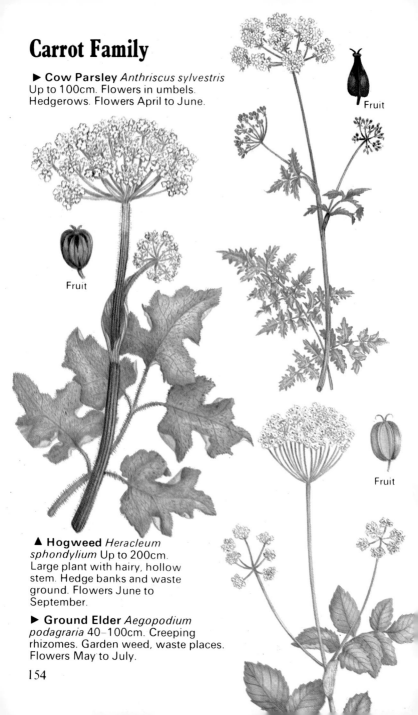

Fruit

Fruit

Fruit

▲ **Hogweed** *Heracleum sphondylium* Up to 200cm.
Large plant with hairy, hollow
stem. Hedge banks and waste
ground. Flowers June to
September.

► **Ground Elder** *Aegopodium podagraria* 40–100cm. Creeping
rhizomes. Garden weed, waste places.
Flowers May to July.

Spurge and Docks

◄ Dog's Mercury *Mercurialis perennis* 15–40cm. This spurge has many flowers in green spikes. Male and female flowers on separate plants. Woodland. Flowers February to April.

◄ Redshank *Polygonum persicaria* 25–75cm. Stems purplish or red. Leaves long and pointed. Many flowers in compact, dense pink head. Arable fields and waste places. Flowers June to October.

Fruit

◄ Common Sorrel *Rumex acetosa* Up to 100cm. Flowers green in loose heads. Male and female flowers on different plants. Fruits green with red edges. Grassland. Flowers May to July.

► Broad-leaved Dock *Rumex obtusifolius* 50–100cm. Green and red flowers in whorls up stem. Fields, waste ground. Weed in pasture. Flowers June to October.

Fruit

Nettle, Heather and Thrift

◄ **Nettle** *Urtica dioica* 30–150cm.
Leaves opposite with sharp teeth and
sharp stinging hairs. Flowers hang in
long spikes. Male and female on
separate plants. Flowers June to
August.

► **Heather** *Calluna
vulgaris* Up to 60cm.
Evergreen leaves are
small, needle-like and
opposite. 4 petals and
4 sepals coloured pale
purple, sometimes
white. Flower in loose
spikes. Heaths and
moors. Flowers July to
September.

► **Bilberry** *Vaccinium
myrtillus* 60cm. Leaves
small, oval. Fruit round,
ripening black. Heaths,
moors. Flowers April to
June.

◄ **Thrift** *Armeria maritima* 5–20cm.
Long, thin leaves form clumps.
Flowers rosy-pink in round head.
Sepals form tube. Coastal marshes,
cliffs. Also on mountains inland.
Flowers April to October.

Primroses and Gentians

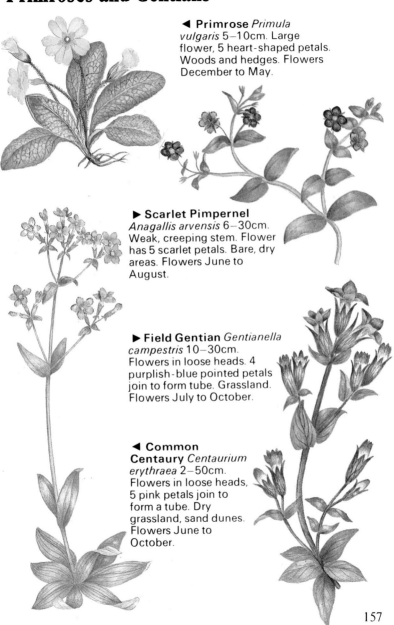

◀ **Primrose** *Primula vulgaris* 5–10cm. Large flower, 5 heart-shaped petals. Woods and hedges. Flowers December to May.

▶ **Scarlet Pimpernel** *Anagallis arvensis* 6–30cm. Weak, creeping stem. Flower has 5 scarlet petals. Bare, dry areas. Flowers June to August.

▶ **Field Gentian** *Gentianella campestris* 10–30cm. Flowers in loose heads. 4 purplish-blue pointed petals join to form tube. Grassland. Flowers July to October.

◀ **Common Centaury** *Centaurium erythraea* 2–50cm. Flowers in loose heads, 5 pink petals join to form a tube. Dry grassland, sand dunes. Flowers June to October.

157

Borage Family

Flower

◀ **Field Forget-me-not**
Myosotis arvensis 15–30cm.
5 bright blue petals, yellow
centre. Roadsides, bare
places. Flowers April to
September.

▶ **Viper's Bugloss**
Echium vulgare 30–
90cm. Flower is pink in
bud, opening to blue. 5
stamens, 4 of which
project beyond flower
with the forked stigma.
Roadsides, dry places.
Flowers June to
September.

Colour
variants

◀ **Common Comfrey**
Symphytum officinale 30–
120cm. Very rough, hairy
plant. Large, pointed leaf
encloses the stem at base.
Many flowers in drooping
heads. Stigma projects
beyond the flower. Damp and
waste places. Flowers May
to June.

Bogbean, Bindweed and Nightshades

▶ **Bogbean** *Menyanthes trifoliata* 15–30cm. Fresh water, damp edges, stems often floating. Flowers May to July.

▼ **Bindweed** *Calystegia sepium* 20–75cm. Climbing stems twine round other plants. Common hedges, waste places. Weed in gardens. Flowers July to September.

▼ **Deadly Nightshade** *Atropa bella-donna* 150cm. Berry black, poisonous. In scrub on chalk soils. Flowers June to August.

Berries

▶ **Bittersweet** *Solanum dulcamara* 30–200cm. 5 narrow, sharply-pointed purple petals. Berries red. Leaves oval with sharp point. Woods, waste ground. Flowers June to September.

Figworts

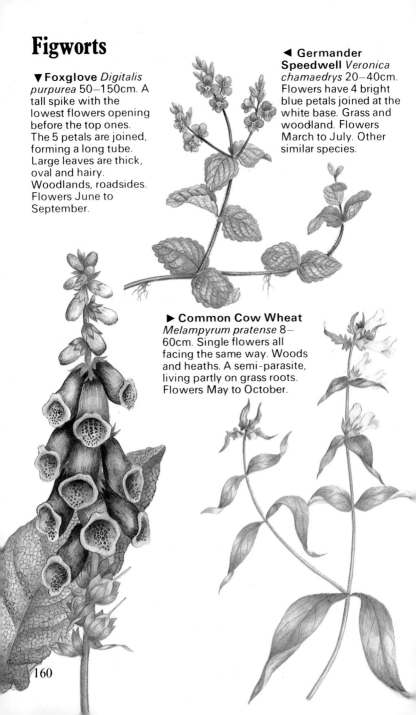

▼**Foxglove** *Digitalis purpurea* 50–150cm. A tall spike with the lowest flowers opening before the top ones. The 5 petals are joined, forming a long tube. Large leaves are thick, oval and hairy. Woodlands, roadsides. Flowers June to September.

◄ **Germander Speedwell** *Veronica chamaedrys* 20–40cm. Flowers have 4 bright blue petals joined at the white base. Grass and woodland. Flowers March to July. Other similar species.

► **Common Cow Wheat** *Melampyrum pratense* 8–60cm. Single flowers all facing the same way. Woods and heaths. A semi-parasite, living partly on grass roots. Flowers May to October.

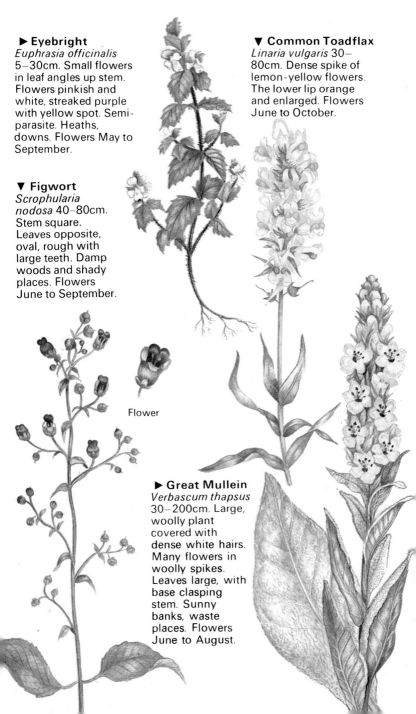

► Eyebright
Euphrasia officinalis
5–30cm. Small flowers in leaf angles up stem. Flowers pinkish and white, streaked purple with yellow spot. Semi-parasite. Heaths, downs. Flowers May to September.

▼ Figwort
Scrophularia nodosa 40–80cm. Stem square. Leaves opposite, oval, rough with large teeth. Damp woods and shady places. Flowers June to September.

Flower

▼ Common Toadflax
Linaria vulgaris 30–80cm. Dense spike of lemon-yellow flowers. The lower lip orange and enlarged. Flowers June to October.

► Great Mullein
Verbascum thapsus 30–200cm. Large, woolly plant covered with dense white hairs. Many flowers in woolly spikes. Leaves large, with base clasping stem. Sunny banks, waste places. Flowers June to August.

Mints, Plantain and Bellflower

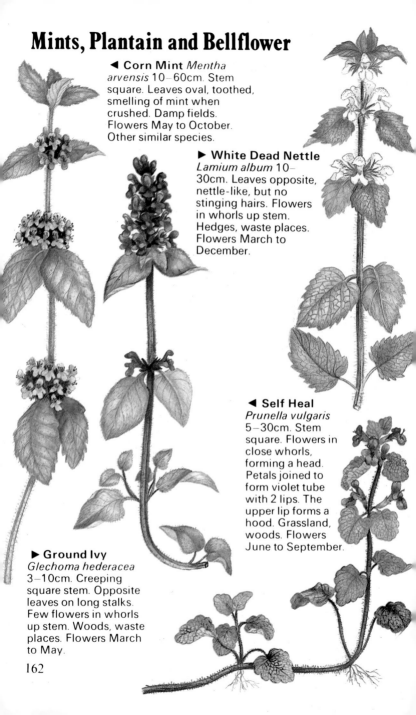

◀ **Corn Mint** *Mentha arvensis* 10–60cm. Stem square. Leaves oval, toothed, smelling of mint when crushed. Damp fields. Flowers May to October. Other similar species.

▶ **White Dead Nettle** *Lamium album* 10–30cm. Leaves opposite, nettle-like, but no stinging hairs. Flowers in whorls up stem. Hedges, waste places. Flowers March to December.

◀ **Self Heal** *Prunella vulgaris* 5–30cm. Stem square. Flowers in close whorls, forming a head. Petals joined to form violet tube with 2 lips. The upper lip forms a hood. Grassland, woods. Flowers June to September.

▶ **Ground Ivy** *Glechoma hederacea* 3–10cm. Creeping square stem. Opposite leaves on long stalks. Few flowers in whorls up stem. Woods, waste places. Flowers March to May.

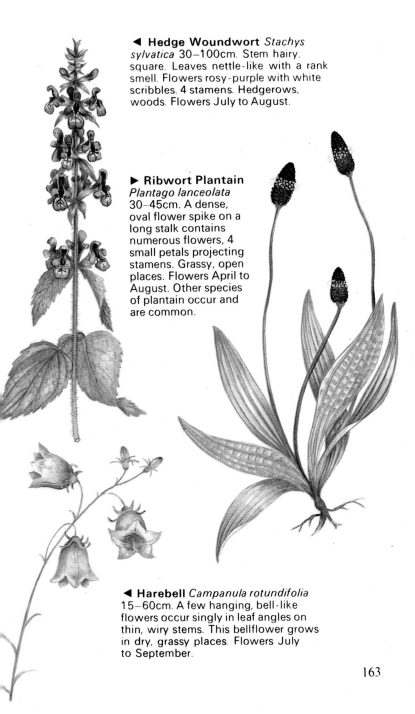

◄ **Hedge Woundwort** *Stachys sylvatica* 30–100cm. Stem hairy, square. Leaves nettle-like with a rank smell. Flowers rosy-purple with white scribbles. 4 stamens. Hedgerows, woods. Flowers July to August.

▶ **Ribwort Plantain** *Plantago lanceolata* 30–45cm. A dense, oval flower spike on a long stalk contains numerous flowers, 4 small petals projecting stamens. Grassy, open places. Flowers April to August. Other species of plantain occur and are common.

◄ **Harebell** *Campanula rotundifolia* 15–60cm. A few hanging, bell-like flowers occur singly in leaf angles on thin, wiry stems. This bellflower grows in dry, grassy places. Flowers July to September.

163

Bedstraws and Honeysuckle

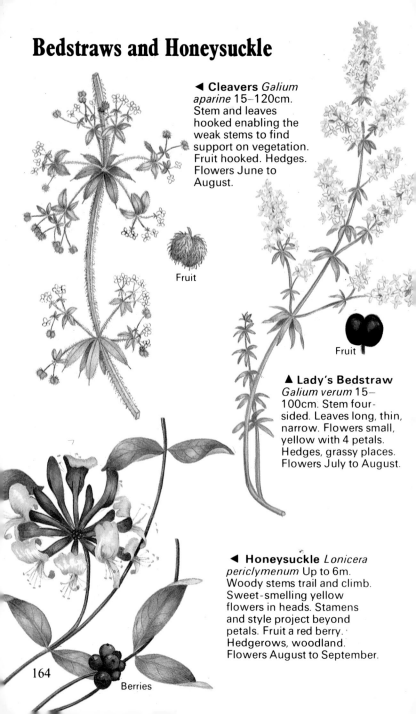

◄ **Cleavers** *Galium aparine* 15–120cm. Stem and leaves hooked enabling the weak stems to find support on vegetation. Fruit hooked. Hedges. Flowers June to August.

Fruit

Fruit

▲ **Lady's Bedstraw** *Galium verum* 15–100cm. Stem four-sided. Leaves long, thin, narrow. Flowers small, yellow with 4 petals. Hedges, grassy places. Flowers July to August.

◄ **Honeysuckle** *Lonicera periclymenum* Up to 6m. Woody stems trail and climb. Sweet-smelling yellow flowers in heads. Stamens and style project beyond petals. Fruit a red berry. Hedgerows, woodland. Flowers August to September.

Berries

164

Scabious and Valerian

► **Field Scabious** *Knautia arvensis*
(far right) 25–100cm. Flowers
numerous in dense head, the largest on
the outside. Purple, with 4 unequal
lilac-blue petals. Dry grassland.
Flowers July to September.

► **Devil's Bit Scabious**
Succisa pratense 15–100cm.
Root short, thick, ending as if
bitten off. Flowers in dense
head, all the same size.
Flowers have 4 petals, 4
stamens. Grassland, woods.
Flowers June to October.

lower

▲ **Common Valerian**
Valeriana officinalis 20–
150cm. Numerous small pale
pink flowers in dense heads.
Leaves divided into many-
lobed leaflets, narrower on
the stem. Earthy smell. Grassy
places and wood edges.
Flowers June to August.

165

Daisy Family

▶ **Daisy** *Bellis perennis*
2–8cm. Numerous flowers
tightly packed into a single
head. Outer ones long, white,
petal-like, sometimes pink-
tipped. Inner flowers short,
tubular, yellow, forming
centre or disc. Grassland.
Flowers March to October.
Ox eye daisy *Chrysanthemum
leucanthemum* 50cm.
Similar. Larger.

▼ **Scentless Mayweed**
Tripleurospermum maritimum
10–30cm. Feathery-looking
foliage. Outer flowers white,
narrow, petal-like. Inner
flowers short tubes forming a
yellow dome in 'flower
centre'. Bare ground. Flowers
July to September.

▼ **Sea Aster** *Aster
tripolium* 15–100cm. Stem·
and leaves fleshy. Leaves
long, narrow. Grows on salt
marshes by sea. Flowers July
to October.

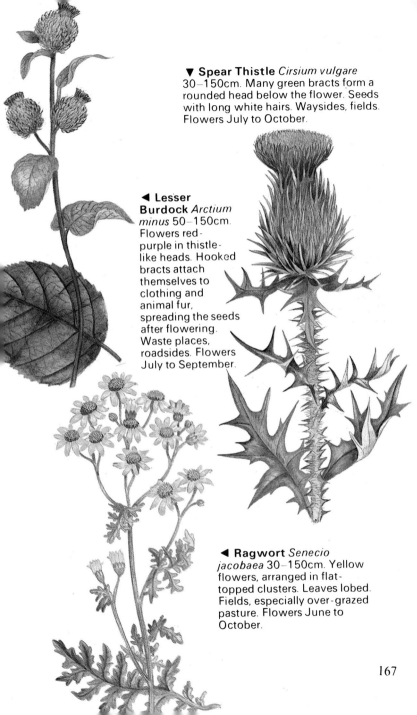

▼ Spear Thistle *Cirsium vulgare*
30–150cm. Many green bracts form a
rounded head below the flower. Seeds
with long white hairs. Waysides, fields.
Flowers July to October.

**◄ Lesser
Burdock** *Arctium
minus* 50–150cm.
Flowers red-
purple in thistle-
like heads. Hooked
bracts attach
themselves to
clothing and
animal fur,
spreading the seeds
after flowering.
Waste places,
roadsides. Flowers
July to September.

◄ Ragwort *Senecio
jacobaea* 30–150cm. Yellow
flowers, arranged in flat-
topped clusters. Leaves lobed.
Fields, especially over-grazed
pasture. Flowers June to
October.

167

Daisy Family

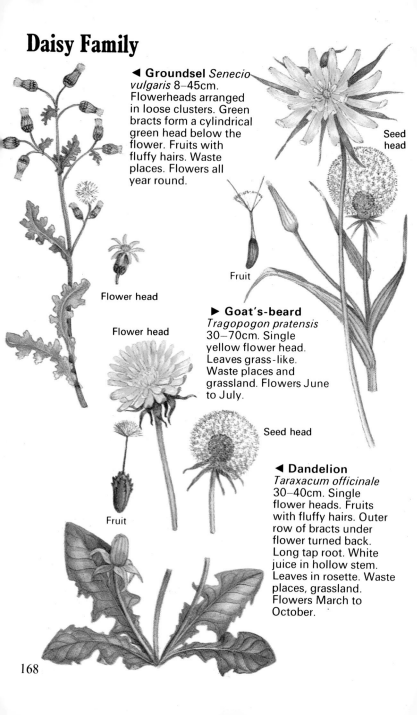

◀ **Groundsel** *Senecio vulgaris* 8–45cm. Flowerheads arranged in loose clusters. Green bracts form a cylindrical green head below the flower. Fruits with fluffy hairs. Waste places. Flowers all year round.

Seed head

Fruit

Flower head

Flower head

▶ **Goat's-beard** *Tragopogon pratensis* 30–70cm. Single yellow flower head. Leaves grass-like. Waste places and grassland. Flowers June to July.

Seed head

Fruit

◀ **Dandelion** *Taraxacum officinale* 30–40cm. Single flower heads. Fruits with fluffy hairs. Outer row of bracts under flower turned back. Long tap root. White juice in hollow stem. Leaves in rosette. Waste places, grassland. Flowers March to October.

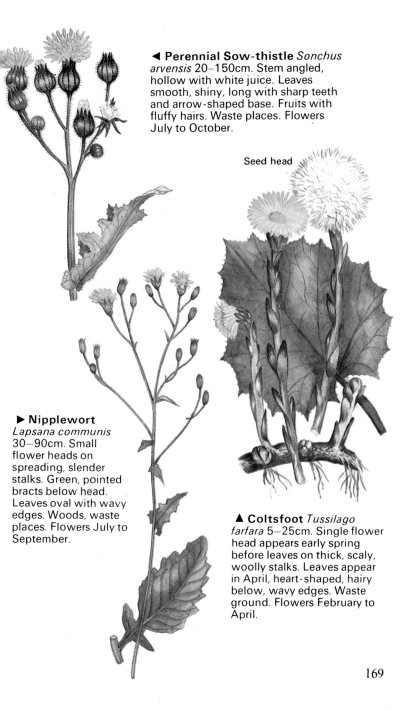

◄ **Perennial Sow-thistle** *Sonchus arvensis* 20–150cm. Stem angled, hollow with white juice. Leaves smooth, shiny, long with sharp teeth and arrow-shaped base. Fruits with fluffy hairs. Waste places. Flowers July to October.

Seed head

▶ **Nipplewort**
Lapsana communis 30–90cm. Small flower heads on spreading, slender stalks. Green, pointed bracts below head. Leaves oval with wavy edges. Woods, waste places. Flowers July to September.

▲ **Coltsfoot** *Tussilago farfara* 5–25cm. Single flower head appears early spring before leaves on thick, scaly, woolly stalks. Leaves appear in April, heart-shaped, hairy below, wavy edges. Waste ground. Flowers February to April.

169

Daisy Family

◄ Butterbur *Petasites hybridus* Up to 150cm. Flowers appear before the leaves in a compact spike. Leaves large and heart-shaped like coltsfoot, but grey hairs below. Wet and damp meadows, river banks, ditches. Flowers March to May.

Flower head

▼ Hemp Agrimony *Eupatorium cannabinum* 30–120cm. Flower heads in rather loose, domed clusters. Opposite leaves, almost stalkless. Marshes, stream sides. Flowers July to September.

▼ Yarrow *Achillea millefolium* 5–15cm. Flowers arranged in flat-topped clusters. Leaves have deeply divided leaflets giving feathery appearance. Meadows, pastures. Flowers June to August.

Flower head

170

Lilies and Arum

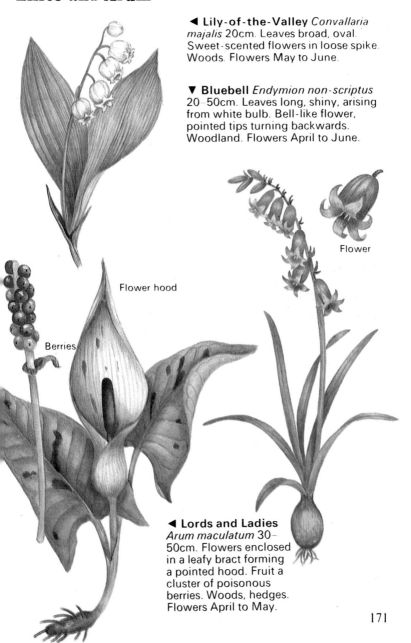

◀ **Lily-of-the-Valley** *Convallaria majalis* 20cm. Leaves broad, oval. Sweet-scented flowers in loose spike. Woods. Flowers May to June.

▼ **Bluebell** *Endymion non-scriptus* 20–50cm. Leaves long, shiny, arising from white bulb. Bell-like flower, pointed tips turning backwards. Woodland. Flowers April to June.

Flower

Flower hood

Berries

◀ **Lords and Ladies** *Arum maculatum* 30–50cm. Flowers enclosed in a leafy bract forming a pointed hood. Fruit a cluster of poisonous berries. Woods, hedges. Flowers April to May.

171

Iris and Daffodils

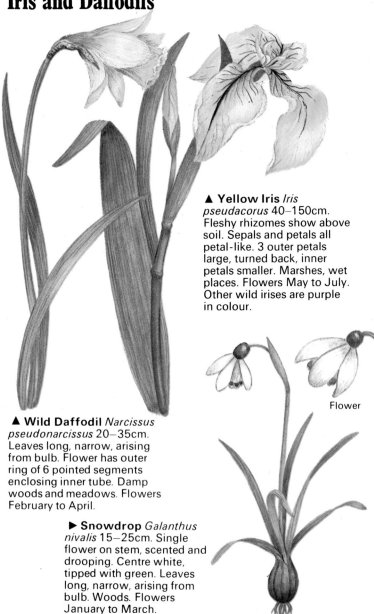

▲ **Yellow Iris** *Iris pseudacorus* 40–150cm. Fleshy rhizomes show above soil. Sepals and petals all petal-like. 3 outer petals large, turned back, inner petals smaller. Marshes, wet places. Flowers May to July. Other wild irises are purple in colour.

Flower

▲ **Wild Daffodil** *Narcissus pseudonarcissus* 20–35cm. Leaves long, narrow, arising from bulb. Flower has outer ring of 6 pointed segments enclosing inner tube. Damp woods and meadows. Flowers February to April.

▶ **Snowdrop** *Galanthus nivalis* 15–25cm. Single flower on stem, scented and drooping. Centre white, tipped with green. Leaves long, narrow, arising from bulb. Woods. Flowers January to March.

Orchids

▶ **Early Purple Orchid** *Orchis mascula* 15–60cm. Many purple flowers in a loose spike. Leaves oval with bases enfolding the stem. Heavily blotched with black spots. Pastures, woods on chalky soils. Flowers April to June.

Flower

▼ **Twayblade** *Listera ovata* 20–60cm. Leaves in pairs at ground level. Many flowers in loose spike. Pasture, woods on chalky soils. Flowers June to July.

Flower

Flower

◀ **Broad-leaved Helleborine** *Epipactis helleborine* 15–50cm. Flowers in spikes. Sepals and petals green or purple. Woods. Flowers July to August.

Rhizome

Mushrooms and Toadstools

Mushrooms and toadstools are the fruit bodies of fungi that consist mainly of white strands in the soil or under the bark or in the wood of trees. These fruit bodies appear only when the fungus is ready to produce spores which are simple 'seeds'. Their function is to carry the spores above the ground so that they will be carried by air currents to new places. There are many different kinds of fungus fruit bodies, but the most commonly seen have a cap which opens out to expose gills or tubes (pores) underneath. These produce large quantities of minute spores. The cap is borne on a stalk and there may be a ring at the top of the stalk where the cap has broken away from it to open. Most fungi produce fruit bodies in the autumn, so September and October are the best months to look for them.

External Features of Fungus Fruit Body with Gills

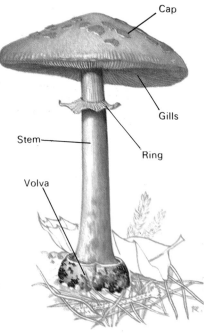

Cap

Gills

Stem

Ring

Volva

CLUES AND HINTS

Where to look: The edges of woodlands and fields are particularly good places to look for a wide variety of species.

Poison: Never pick or eat a mushroom until you are absolutely certain that it is not poisonous.

▼ **Beefsteak Fungus** *Fistulina hepatica* 5–30cm. Red-brown, hoof-shaped, growing rapidly in late summer on oak trees.

Fungi with Gills

◄ Fly Agaric *Amanita muscaria* Cap 6–16cm, red with white patches. Gills white. Stem white with ring and bulbous base. Occurs in birch woods. POISONOUS.

► Death Cap *Amanita phalloides* Cap 7–12cm, olive or yellowish-green and indistinctly streaky. Gills white. Stem white or yellow-green with ring and cup-like volva at base. Found in leafy woods, especially with oak. Extremely POISONOUS, usually fatal.

► Tawny Grisette *Amanita fulva* Cap 4–7cm, orange or tawny, acorn-shaped then flat with raised darker centre, and piecrust edge. Gills white. Stem tall, fragile with sack-like volva but no ring. Woodlands. Edible.

▼ Parasol Mushroom *Lepiota procera* Cap 10–20cm, becoming flat with central boss. Gills white. Stem tall with ring. Broadleaved woodland clearings and pastures. Edible.

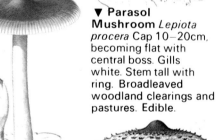

◄ Shaggy Parasol *Lepiota rhacodes* Cap 8–15cm. Like parasol mushroom but shorter, sturdy, lacks scales on stem and cut flesh turns red. Central boss flattened. Shady woods and gardens. Edible.

Fungi with Gills

◀ **Poached Egg Fungus** *Oudemansiella mucida* Cap 3–8cm, slimy, white or with greyish tint. Gills widely spaced and white. Stem thin, firm, with ring. Clustered on trunks of dead and dying beech trees in autumn. Edible but not recommended.

▲ **Honey Fungus** *Armillaria mellea* Cap 3–10cm, tawny with darker scales. Stem honey-coloured with cottony ring. Gills whitish. Kills many trees and shrubs. Common. Edible when young.

◀ **Horn of Plenty** *Craterellus cornucopioides* Cap 9cm, hollow, funnel-shaped with wavy margin. Outside uneven, smoky-grey; inside felty, grey-brown. In clusters on ground. Edible.

▶ **Chanterelle** *Cantharellus cibarius* Cap 3–10cm, cone-shaped, apricot or egg-yellow. Gills irregularly branched, fold-like, running down stem. Broadleaved woods. Edible.

▶ **Saffron Milk Cap** *Lactarius deliciosus* Cap 4–10cm, concave, orange-red, staining green. Gills exuding carrot-coloured juice when broken. Under coniferous trees. Edible.

▼ **Ugly Milk Cap** *Lactarius turpis* Cap 6–14cm, olive-brown, margin yellowish. Gills yellow-brown, exuding white 'milk' when cut. Under birch trees. Inedible.

▶ **Clouded Agaric** *Clitocybe nebularis* Cap 6–15cm, flattened, ash-grey. Stem stout, lighter. Gills whitish. Occurs in woods. Indigestible.

◀ **The Sickener** *Russula emetica* Cap 6–9cm, shiny scarlet, becoming concave. Flesh peppery. Gills white. Under conifers and beech. Causes vomiting.

▶ **Velvet Shank** *Flammulina velutipes* Cap 2–6cm, yellowish, slimy. Stem dark brown velvety. Gills pale yellow. In winter on trunks and branches. Edible.

Fungi with Gills

◄ Amethyst Deceiver *Laccaria amethystea* Cap 2–3cm. Like *L. laccata* but entirely dark violet when moist, drying buff with lilac tint. Edible.

▼ Spindle Shank *Collybia fusipes* Cap 3–8cm, reddish-brown or liver-coloured. Gills whitish, often spotted. Stem red-brown, grooved. Tufted at base of oak and beech. Edible.

▲ Wood Blewit *Lepista nuda*. At first entirely lilac or violet. Cap 6–10cm, becoming brownish with age. Gills crowded, violet, fading when old. Woods. Edible.

► Deceiver *Laccaria laccata* Cap 1–4cm. Cap and stem reddish-brown when moist, drying buff. Gills thick, uneven, flesh-coloured. Stem tough. Variable in form. Common. Edible.

◄ Fairy-ring Champignon *Marasmius oreades* Cap 2–6cm, pink, tan or buff, with central boss. Gills pale, widely spaced. In short grass; often in fairy rings. Edible.

▶ St George's Mushroom
Tricholoma gambosum
Cap 5–15cm, thick, fleshy, whitish. Gills white, crowded. Stem thick, swollen at base. Flesh has mealy smell. Amongst grass in spring. Edible.

▲ *Hygrophorus coccineus* (No common name) At first entirely scarlet, fading yellowish. Cap moist, 2–5cm, domed. Gills waxy. In grass. Edible.

▶ Milking Mycena
Mycena galopus Cap to 1.5cm, conical, grey with darker centre and radiating lines. Stem similar exuding white 'milk' when broken. Gills white. Amongst dead leaves in autumn. Inedible.

◀ Oyster Fungus
Pleurotus ostreatus
Cap 3–15cm, blue-grey then fawn, fan or shell-shaped. Attached to tree trunks by stalk at one side. Gills whitish, running down stem. Edible but tough.

179

Fungi with Gills

◀ **Common Pluteus** *Pluteus cervinus* Cap 3–8cm, sooty brown or umber, becoming flattened. Gills pinkish, free. Stem white, streaked below with brown fibrils. Edible.

▼ *Gymnopilus junonius* (No common name) Cap 6–12cm, rounded, golden-brown, scaly. Stem similar with ring. Gills rust-coloured, crowded. Tufted at base of trunks. Inedible.

▼ *Pholiota aurivella* (No common name) Cap 5–12cm, glutinous, deep yellow with concentric chestnut scales. Stem light yellow with temporary ring and brown scales below. Gills becoming rust-coloured. Inedible.

▼ **Shaggy Pholiota** *Pholiota squarrosa* Cap 3–8cm, rounded, straw-coloured, densely covered with upturned scales. Stem similarly scaly. Edible, but very tough.

◀ *Cortinarius pseudosalor* (No common name) Cap 3–7cm, conical, glutinous, buff-coloured. Stem short, pointed, white above, lilac and glutinous below ring zone. Gills buff, edged in lilac. Edible.

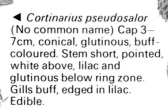

◀ *Inocybe geophylla* (No common name) Cap 2cm, white, silky, bell-shaped then flattened with central boss. Gills becoming clay-brown. Stem slender, white. Lilac variety (right) *I.g.* var. *lilacina*. POISONOUS.

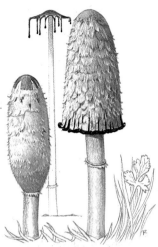

▼ **Field Mushroom** *Agaricus campestris* Cap 4–8cm, smooth, white or brownish. Stem short, slight ring. Gills deep pink then purplish-brown. Flesh white or brownish. Occurs in fields. Edible.

▲ **Shaggy Ink Cap** *Coprinus comatus* Cap 5–12cm long. Cylindrical then bell-shaped, white, shaggy. Stem tall with ring. Gills finally black and dissolving into inky fluid. Fields and rubbish dumps. Edible.

◀ **Sulphur Tuft** *Hypholoma fasciculare* Cap 3–7cm, bright sulphur yellow, centre darker. Stem slender, yellow, no ring. Gills sulphur yellow, becoming olive. POISONOUS.

▶ **Verdigris Fungus** *Stropharia aeruginosa* Cap 2–8cm, blue-green, slimy, convex, flecked with white scales. Stem stout, paler, scaly below ring. Inedible.

181

Fungi with Tubes

◀ *Suillus grevillei* (No common name) Cap 5–12cm, slimy, yellow. Stem darker with ring. Occurs in coniferous woods. Edible.

▶ **Orange Cap Boletus** *Leccinum versipelle* Cap 8–20cm, hemispherical, orange or brick-red. Stem robust with black dots. Found in pastures and woods. Edible.

▶ **Cep** *Boletus edulis* Cap 6–20cm, bun-like, warm brown. Stem swollen, pale brown with whitish network of veins. Pores white or yellow-green. Woodlands. Edible.

▼ **Dryad's Saddle** *Polyporus squamosus* Cap 10–30cm, fan-shaped, buff with brown scales. Stem off-centre. On trees. Edible.

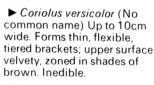

▲ **Birch Bracket** *Piptoporus betulinus* 10–20cm wide. Smooth, greyish, hoof-shaped. Confined to birch. Inedible.

▶ *Coriolus versicolor* (No common name) Up to 10cm wide. Forms thin, flexible, tiered brackets; upper surface velvety, zoned in shades of brown. Inedible.

Other Fungi

▶ *Hydnum repandum* (No common name) Cap 5–12cm, fleshy, convex, pinkish-buff with crowded spines beneath. Stem white. Deciduous woodlands. Edible.

◀ *Clavulina cristata* (No common name) 3–8cm high, forming branched, white, coral-like tufts. On ground in woods. Edible, but best avoided.

▼ **Jew's Ear** *Auricularia auricula-judae* 3–10cm. Helmet-shaped with ear-like folds beneath. Light brown, flabby and gelatinous with velvety surface. Edible.

▲ **Earth Star** *Geastrum triplex* Up to 10cm wide. Spore sac sitting in saucer-like portion. Deciduous woodland. Inedible.

▼ **Common Earth-ball** *Scleroderma citrinum* 4–8cm wide. Rounded, yellowish, scaly. Interior purplish-black. Found on sandy heaths and woodland. Inedible.

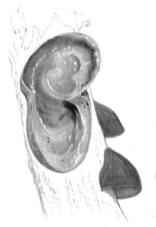

Index

184

ACKNOWLEDGEMENTS

The publishers wish to thank the following people for their help in supplying artwork and photographs for this book:

Artwork: Norma Birgin, Wendy Bramall, Terry Callcut, Martin Camm, Bernard Robinson, Rod Sutterby, David Wright.

Photographs: Heather Angel 65, 73; Joe Blossom/NHPA 6; Michael Chinery 60; Stephen Dalton/NHPA 4; Sonia Halliday 104 top right; Brian Hawkes/NHPA 60, 89, Ken Merrylees 104 top centre, bottom left and right; Maurice Nimmo 5, 104 bottom centre.

Picture Research: Penny Warn.